STATISTICAL APPLICATIONS IN LIBRARY TECHNICAL SERVICES:
AN ANNOTATED BIBLIOGRAPHY

edited by Sue A. Burkholder

prepared by LAMA, Statistics Section, Task Force:
Statistical Applications in Technical Services
Linda S. Vertrees, chairperson
Edward Bachus, Julianne Beall, Sue A. Burkholder,
Lawrence Heilos, Elizabeth Hood, Shirley Leung,
Katha Massey, Susan Phillips and Suzanne Striedieck

Library Administration and Management Association
American Library Association
Chicago
1987

Statistical Applications in Library Technical Services:
An Annotated Bibliography (1987)

Published by the Library Administration and Management Association
a division of the American Library Association
50 East Huron Street
Chicago, Illinois 60611

Z
688.5
.S83
1987

ISBN: 0-8389-7086-9

Copyright © 1987 by the American Library Association. All rights
reserved except those which may be granted by Sections 107 and 108 of the
Copyright Revision Act of 1976. Printed in the United States of America.

STATISTICAL APPLICATIONS IN LIBRARY TECHNICAL SERVICES:
AN ANNOTATED BIBLIOGRAPHY

TABLE OF CONTENTS

Page

Introduction v
List of Annotated Journals xi

1. Technical Services 1
   General and Miscellaneous 1
   Automation 3
   Productivity and Cost Statistics 7
2. Acquisitions 13
   General and Miscellaneous 13
   Approval Plans 19
   Automation 22
   Gifts and Exchange 23
   Materials Budget 25
   Vendor Performance 39
3. Serials 45
   General and Miscellaneous 45
   Automation 60
   Costs 61
4. Cataloging 67
   General and Miscellaneous 67
   Authority Control 77
   Automation 80
   Retrospective Conversion 88
5. Catalog Structure and Use 91
   General and Miscellaneous 91
   Card Catalogs 94
   COM Catalogs 97
   Online Catalogs 99
6. Collection Development, Analysis and Management 107
   General and Miscellaneous 107
   Analysis of Holdings 117
   Collection Management 128
   Loss Rate 135
   Shelving 139
   Use Patterns 141

TABLE OF CONTENTS CONT'D.

Page

7. Preservation/Conservation 157
    General and Miscellaneous 157
    Binding 158
    Reprography 159
    Shelf Preparation 160
8. Miscellaneous and Other Articles 161

    Indexes 165
    Author 165
    Key Word 173

Statistical Applications in Library Technical Services:
An Annotated Bibliography

Introduction

For centuries, libraries have described themselves at least partially in terms of numbers: numbers of books owned, numbers of books added, copies made (even hand-made transcripts) and numbers of books withdrawn, sold to other libraries, lost, and so forth. More recently, most units of library administration have quantified not only these activities but many others as well. A great deal of this statistical effort has centered on library technical services. Every library technical services unit counts some elements of its work, and most units count extensively. This statistical effort has been utilized in library administration, planning, and research. It has been augmented by compilations of the data of many libraries and by research based on specially designed statistical criteria.

PURPOSE

This bibliography addresses the published results of this burgeoning body of statistical information on library technical services. It covers the period from 1975-1985. Its purpose is to collect in a useful reference work bibliographic sources for the aid of practitioners and researchers in statistical applications in technical services. Primarily, the citations listed consist of practical applications, as opposed to theoretical descriptions of statistical applications. It is hoped that the bibliography will encourage the collection of relevant data, increase the effective use of that data in practical library applications, stimulate a broadening of the scope of statistical research applications in library and information science, and foster an increased appreciation of the complexity of questions of bibliographic access and control.

AUDIENCE

The compilers of this bibliography anticipate that a number of different constituents will be found among its audience. The bibliography is intended for all technical services librarians in all types of libraries. It is hoped that technical services practitioners, technical services managers, and collection development librarians might find much of interest and utility in the bibliography. Additionally, public services librarians concerned with the impact of technical services upon the whole of library service might find topics to engage their attention. Library administrators might well make use of statistical data and applications techniques covered by the articles cited. Additionally, we anticipate that students and professors of library and information science will find the bibliography helpful. While some citations might apply to a particular type or size of library, the techniques used can be generalized, and the examples of data use for planning and decision making are potentially of interest to all. The reader need not have much statistical background to make good use of the bibliography, although there are some articles which employ advanced statistical techniques.

SCOPE

Although many of the lines between technical and public services have blurred recently, this study defines technical services in rather traditional yet broad categories. For the purposes of this bibliography, technical services encompasses acquisitions; serials; cataloging; catalog structure and use; collection development, analysis and management; and preservation and conservation. One might wonder why some topics were included and others not. Certain aspects of collection management which deal heavily with file management and bibliographic data are not included, namely circulation and interlibrary loan. On the other hand, a rather comprehensive definition of collection development has been adopted, as well as of catalog use. The decision whether to include an article was sometimes a difficult one. Generally speaking, those library functions are included which are usually carried out without direct contact between a library staff member and user.

The bibliography focuses upon the functional categories falling within its definition of technical services. These broad subjects are arranged as chapters and are subdivided further. A list of journals examined is included at the end of this introduction.

This bibliography is not intended to be a comprehensive compilation of bibliographic citations, but rather a reflection of the major body of periodical literature on statistical applications in technical services. It includes all pertinent articles from the major library journals in which there is significant coverage of technical services. For the most part, monographic literature is not covered. The articles cited and abstracted cover some quantitative aspect of technical services work. This includes works both of and about statistics in technical services. Articles on statistics applied to general librarianship have been excluded, as have those of an instructional or theoretical nature on statistics in general. The rare exceptions to this rule are basic introductions to statistical methods relevant but not restricted to technical services applications and found in the journals under review.

Although the bibliography is not comprehensive for the topic under consideration, it is comprehensive for the journals reviewed. Therefore, it is not evaluative in terms of articles included. Furthermore, the annotations which accompany the citations are descriptive, not evaluative. We believe that even poor methodology or techniques can be instructive and that a negative comment about a study would discourage readership of an article which might be valuable, even if flawed. Therefore, users of this bibliography will need to develop their own value standards based on their own purposes, as their understanding of statistical applications expands.

METHOD OF COMPILATION AND ARRANGEMENT

The citations in this bibliography were compiled by examining significant journals in the area of technical services to discover articles in the following main categories: description of the methods of statistics utilization in technical services management, reports of statistics gathering and use by individual libraries, reports of collections of statistics, and statistical applications in technical services research. The decision of the Task Force was to be more inclusive than exclusive. In addition to journal articles, ERIC was searched under appropriate terms. Each article or monograph in the resulting list was examined, and the same four categories of work are included.

All citations were abstracted by contributors to the bibliography. Each citation was assigned to one or more subject groupings based on the broad functions included within the scope of "technical services" and/or within function subdivisions. The citations and abstracts were then compiled by categories. Therefore, some articles appear in more than one chapter or subdivision. Within chapter sections, citations are arranged in reverse chronological order and subarranged alphabetically by author. The citations are indexed by author and by keyword/subject.

The types of citations included in the subject-oriented chapters reveal much about the directions of research in librarianship. Occasionally, the lack of material on a given subject might reveal the quandry of the profession in the face of a problem not yet addressed successfully.

The chapter on general Technical Services includes articles on statistical methods, staffing, and consolidation of technical services units. Surprisingly, more statistics-based work was published in the late 1970's than recently on automation, particularly with regard to system or equipment selection. More recent articles on automation are concerned with costs, performance, and statistical methods. The chapter sub-heading on Productivity and Cost Studies reveals an emphasis on total processing operations or segments of the processing operation, but some deal with specific type of material, e.g., serials and monographs.

The chapter on Acquisitions covers a broad range of topics. Many articles in this chapter are cross-listed in other chapters. Relatively few citations describe in-house operations. Some of the more frequently analyzed topics are serials acquisitions, bibliographic searching, and indicators for purchase. The section on approval plans deals primarily with vendor selection and evaluation, but occasionally with other topics, such as comparisons with other purchasing methods. There is very little on acquisitions automation, either function specific or integrated systems. The Gifts and Exchange section deals mainly with two areas, cost effectiveness and international exchange. Notably absent are articles on the application of automation to gifts and exchange procedures.

By far the largest section of the Acquisitions chapter is the sub-chapter devoted to the Materials Budget. There is heavy emphasis on the cost of serials, especially higher prices for U. S. libraries or for institutions. Other topics encountered are budget allocation procedures, price indexes and analyses of their use, and methods of coping with inflated materials prices. There are a number of citations from non-U. S. sources in this section. The Acquisitions sub-chapter on Vendor Performance deals again with approval plans, but more specifically with publishers, distributors, book vendors, and serials subscription agents.

The chapter on Serials includes much on serials collection development and on evaluation of serial and periodical use. A related question, criteria for selection and de-selection, also receives emphasis, as well as the relationship of use to the total cost of ownership. Interlibrary loan and other cooperative approaches, while not missing altogether, are not prominent. Somewhat surprisingly, few articles cited deal with procedural aspects of serial routines or other costs. The brief sub-chapter on Automation includes general reviews of both integrated library systems with serials components and with systems devoted to the serials function. The section on Costs includes subscription costs, cost-effectiveness of subscription agent services, price indexes, discrepant pricing structures, and predictably, inflation.

The chapter on Cataloging covers a variety of cataloging topics, from overall cataloging procedures, to specialized cataloging questions to personnel and education issues. In the years prior to and following 1981, there are reviews of studies of the impact of AACR 2. The sub-chapter on Authority Control emphasizes the on-line environment, comparisons between computer-based and manual systems, and AACR 2. There are some articles on subject authority control as well. The section on Automation deals almost exclusively with shared catalog data sources, not individual library automation studies. Utilities and other data sources, use patterns of bibliographic networks, quality control, costs analyses, search strategies, and availability of copy are conspicuous. Most articles cited in the sub-chapters on Retrospective Conversion describe "retro" projects at one or more libraries, but some are concerned with quality control or justification for retrospective conversion.

The Catalog Structure and Use chapter addresses questions of catalog format chiefly. Articles on other aspects of catalog use are present, notably subject specific use, the relationship of access points to use indicators such as circulation, fullness of bibliographic record, physical maintenance, and costs. The General and Miscellaneous section of the chapter includes comparisons among catalog formats (e.g., microform and on-line) and the three sub-chapters on the Card Catalog, COM Catalog, and On-line Catalog treat format-specific studies in greater depth. Although there are recurring topics in all three sub-chapters there are more citations of studies of search strategies and catalog maintenance in the Card Catalog section; more studies of split files (closed catalogs, etc.) in the COM Catalog section; and more articles on authority systems, search formulation and indexing (field specific and key-word), and a bit on record structure in the On-line section.

With 230 citations, the bibliography's most extensive Chapter is Collection Development, Analysis, and Management. As might be expected many of the articles are cross-listed in the Acquisitions chapter. Throughout the chapter's subheadings are a large number of articles dealing specifically with serials also. There are papers analyzing selection criteria, allocation formulas, decision models, citation analysis, and growth rates. The Analysis of Holdings sub-chapter includes articles analyzing individual libraries' holdings and subject area holdings, comparisons and coordination of collection development among libraries, core collections, sampling techniques, the use of bibliographic utility archive tapes as an information source, and other automated techniques. The Collection Management sub-chapter includes articles on bibliometric applications, modelling techniques for weeding and storage, the "Bradford distribution," and the use of mainframe and micro computers for analysis. The section also contains articles on use, cost, and retention of serials; circulation analysis; literature identification for subject area building; and inventory. The subchapter on Loss Rate cites research on methods of maintaining loss records, mutilation patterns, inventory (including automated applications), and security systems. The brief shelving section reports studies of shelving workload, shelf-reading, needs projections, and misshelving models.

The substantial sub-chapter on Use Patterns includes perhaps the most statistically sophisticated techniques in the bibliography. There are applications of predictive use modelling, use patterns as they relate to catalog entries, citation analyses of research by faculty and students, core collection analyses, and browsing behavior. Several articles study circulation statistics, interlibrary loan, and circulation availability as indicators of use. Some studies are discipline oriented or make interdisciplinary comparisons. There are a number of articles on serial use based on use per title, per foot of shelf space, and per monetary unit. Several studies use data generated by automated systems, but not many rely on computer analysis of the data.

The chapter on Preservation/Conservation might well have been called "The Unsolved Problem." The chapter is predictably and unfortunately brief, since few libraries or librarians have begun addressing the conservation/preservation problem despite its pervasive presence. However, the studies in the chapter might provide a useful starting point for studying a preservation/conservation program. Cited are papers on deterioration rates and selection of titles for conservation and restoration.

The final chapter of the bibliography, Miscellaneous and Other Articles, cites statistical methods of relevance to studies in library technical services chiefly.

The members of the Task Force hope that their work will prove valuable to the library community, and that the information included here might be brought up-to-date by similar compilations from time to time.

List of Annotated Journals

Advances in Librarianship, vol. 5-13 (1975-1984)
ALA Yearbook, vol. 1-8 (1976-1983)
ALA Yearbook of Library and Information Services, vol. 9-10 (1984-1985)
American Libraries, vol. 6-16 (1975-1985)
American Society for Information Science Proceedings, vol. 12-22 (1975-1985)
Annual Review of Information Science and Technology, vol. 10-20 (1975-1985)
Aslib Proceedings, vol. 27-37 (1975-1985)
Australian Academic and Research Libraries, vol. 6-16 (1975-1985)
Australian Library Journal, vol. 24-34 (1975-1985)
Bowker Annual of Library and Book Trade Information, vol. 20-30 (1975-1985)
Canadian Library Journal, vol. 32-42 (1975-1985)
Cataloging and Classification Quarterly, vol. 1-6 (1980-1985)
Catholic Library World, vol. 47-56 (1975-1985)
Clinic on Library Applications of Data Processing. Proceedings, 1975-1984
Collection Management, vol. 1-7 (1976-1985)
College and Research Libraries, vol. 36-46 (1975-1985)
De-acquisitions Librarian, vol. 1, 1976
Drexel Library Quarterly, vol. 11-21, no. 1 (1975-1985)
ERIC online database, 1975-1985
Illinois Libraries, vol. 1-2 (1978-1980)
Information Processing and Management, vol. 11-21 (1975-1985)
Information Retrieval & Library Automation, vol. 11-15 (1975-1979)
Information Technology and Libraries, vol. 1-4 (1982-1985)
Journal of Academic Librarianship, vol. 1-10 (1975-1985)
Journal of Library Automation, vol. 8-14 (1975-1981)
Journal of the American Society for Information Science, vol. 26-36 (1975-1985)
Library Acquisitions, vol. 1-9, (1977-1985)
Library and Archival Security, vol. 2, no. 3/4 (1978-1985)
Library and Information Science Research, vol. 5-7 (1983-1985)
Library Association Record, vol. 77-87 (1975-1985)
Library Journal, vol. 100-110 (1975-1985)
Library Quarterly, vol. 45-55 (1975-1985)
Library Research, vol. 1-4 (1979-1982)
Library Resources and Technical Services, vol. 19-29 (1975-1985)
Library Review, vol. 25-34 (1975/76-1985)
Library Security Newsletter, vol. 1-2, no. 2 (1975-1978)
Library Trends, vol. 24-33 (1975-1985)
Libri, vol. 25-35 (1975-1985)
New Zealand Libraries, vol. 38-44 (1975-1985)
Ohio Library Association Bulletin, vol. 45-55 (1975-1985)
ONLINE, vol. 1-9 (1977-1985)
Public Libraries, vol. 17-24 (1978-1985)
Public Library Quarterly, vol. 1-6 (1979-1985)
Serials Librarian, vol. 1-9 (1976-1985)
Southeastern Librarian, vol. 25-35 (1975-1985)
Special Libraries, vol. 66-76 (1975-1985)
Technical Services Quarterly, vol. 1-2 (1983-1985)
Wilson Library Bulletin, vol. 50-60 (1975-1985)

CHAPTER 1

TECHNICAL SERVICES

GENERAL AND MISCELLANEOUS

University of Melbourne. Library. Working Group. "Part-time Work Patterns in Some Melbourne Academic Libraries." <u>Australian Academic and Research Libraries</u> 14 (December 1983): 229-234.

A1

Abstract: Presents results of a survey of six academic libraries in Melbourne on use of permanent part-time staff. Gives proportion of total staff that are permanent part time. Includes comparison of use by function: reader services, technical services, other.

Graham, Peter S. "Technical Services Costs in ARL Libraries. SPEC Kit 89." 1982. ERIC ED232670. Microfiche.

A2

Abstract: Summarizes data from 81 respondents to a survey of ARL libraries on technical services costs. Appended are reports from seven libraries, including statistical compilations and other supporting documents on technical services cost studies.

Iehl, Ronald E. and Edward John Kazlauskas. "Use of SPSS to Enhance Management Decision Making." <u>American Society for Information Science Proceedings</u> 19 (1982): 141-143.

A3

Abstract: Describes how SPSS is used in a large university library to analyze vendor performance, monitor processing times and provide other technical processing management reports.

Robinson, Earl J. and Stephen J. Turner. "Improving Library Effectiveness: A Proposal for Applying Fuzzy Set Concepts in the Management of Large Collections." <u>Journal of the American Society for Information Science</u> 32 (November 1981): 458-462.

A4

Abstract: Introduces a mathematical modeling concept called fuzzy set theory to library managers. Describes the theory and its development and proposes an approach to its application in libraries.

Bryan, Harrison. "Australian Academic Libraries--Projections from the Past." <u>Australian Academic and Research Libraries</u> 11 (June 1980): 96-110.

A5

<u>Abstract</u>: Gives published statistics for Australian academic libraries, measures them against various standards, and makes tentative projections for the future. Statistics relevant to technical services include book stock, books per reader, technical services staff, and ratio of technical services staff to number of volumes accessioned.

Heinritz, Fred J. "Decision Tables: A Tool for Librarians." <u>Library Resources and Technical Services</u> 21 (Winter 1978): 42-46.

A6

<u>Abstract</u>: The decision table is a valuable aid in describing, understanding, and improving both manual and automated library procedures. An explanation of how these tables are made and used is given, with several examples and a bibliography.

Fry, James W. "A Feasibility Study for Consolidating and/or Coordinating Technical Procedures in Beaver County, Pennsylvania Libraries." 1977.

A7 ERIC ED148363. Microfiche.

<u>Abstract</u>: This study analyzed for public, school, academic and special libraries in Beaver County, Pennsylvania, existing library material purchasing procedures, cataloging practices, and processing methods and made recommendations on the feasibility of consolidating or coordinating such activities.

Brock, Joan, Doris Paterson and Patricia Alexander. "Survey of Current Staffing Practice in Public Libraries." <u>New Zealand Libraries</u> 38

A8 (April 1975): 74-85.

<u>Abstract</u>: Reports on a survey of New Zealand public libraries about staffing practice, and measures that practice against New Zealand Library Association standards for number and qualifications of staff. Covers all staff, but has breakdowns for catalogers and for commercial and technical librarians.

Burns, Robert W. "An Investigation Into the Feasibility of Merging Three Technical Processing Operations Into One Central Unit." (August 1974) ERIC ED100341. Microfiche.

A9

Abstract: Report of a study undertaken to examine the feasibility of merging the technical services units of three academic libraries into one administrative unit. Differences in accounting procedures and State fiscal policies are mentioned as a major hindrance to such a merger.

Rouse, William B. "Optimal Resource Allocation in Library Systems." *Journal of the American Society for Information Science* 26 (May-June 1975): 157-165.

A10

Abstract: Develops and discusses a general procedure for optimal allocation of resources among the many processes of a library system. Could be applied to technical services.

Tuttle, Helen Welch. "Coordination of the Technical Services." *Advances in Librarianship* 5 (1975): 123-146.

A11

Abstract: Review article that discusses the coordination role of the head of technical services in larger libraries. One section examines the standardization of library statistics.

AUTOMATION

Busch, B. J. "Automation and Reorganization of Technical Services. SPEC Kit 112." 1985. ERIC ED256370. Microfiche.

A12

Abstract: Report of a 1984 survey of the 117 Association of Research Libraries (ARL) members to determine the extent of staff reorganization based on the capabilities of automated systems. Contains statistical results of survey and supporting documents from several ARL institutions.

Getz, Malcolm and Doug Phelps. "Labor Costs in the Technical Operation of Three Research Libraries." *Journal of Academic Librarianship* 10 (September 1984): 209-219.

A13

Abstract: Cost studies of technical services operations in three middle-sized research libraries. The focus of the studies was on costs of labor and the effects of automation.

Dowlin, Kenneth E. "The Use of Standard Statistics in an On-line Library Management System." <u>Public Library Quarterly</u> 3 (Spring/Summer 1982): 37-46.

A14

<u>Abstract</u>: General discussion of the types of materials processing and production statistics that can be generated by an integrated library system. These can then be used as the basis for a decision support system to provide assistance in daily decision making.

Lundeen, Gerald W. and Charles H. Davis, "Library Automation." <u>Annual Review of Information Science and Technology</u> 17 (1982): 161-186.

A15

<u>Abstract</u>: Review article covering the years 1980 and 1981 which looks at library automation. Sections on the technical services are included.

Williams, Martha E. and others. "MARC Database Statistics: An Aid to BSDP Participants Covering Volumes 1 through 8 of the LC MARC Database BOOKS ALL. Final Report." 1982. ERIC ED234782. Microfiche.

A16

<u>Abstract</u>: Analysis of MARC records from 1973 to 1981 based on record length, field of occurrence, data element length per field tag, and classification by Dewey Decimal or Library of Congress schedule. Extensive tables. Data may prove useful to planners of machine-readable catalog files and MARC file users.

Lawton, Stephen B. "Diffusion of Automation in Post-secondary Institutions." <u>Canadian Library Journal</u> 38 (April 1981): 93-97.

A17

<u>Abstract</u>: Analysis of the results of a survey to determine the pattern of diffusion of library automation in Canadian educational institutions. Covers ordering, cataloging, COM catalogs, online catalogs, circulation, item identification, and commercial database searching.

Mick, Colin K. "Cost analysis of Information Systems and Services." <u>Annual Review of Information Science and Technology</u> 14 (1979): 37-64.

A18

<u>Abstract</u>: Article reviewing representative key studies published between 1975 and 1979 dealing with cost analysis of information systems and services. A number of studies relating to technical services are included.

Ross, Ryburn M. "Cost Analysis of Automation in Technical Services." In
    The Economics of Library Automation, 1976 Clinic on Library
    Applications of Data Processing, pp. 10-27. Urbana: University of
A19 Illinois Graduate School of Library and Information Science, 1977.

Abstract: Develops costs for automation activities, with specific
information on cataloging costs before and after automation. Presents
some information on productivity measurement and proposes techniques
to measure technical services staff performance.

Shoemaker, Thomas P. "Public Library Automation Network: A Cost/Benefit
    Analysis of the PLAN Project." 1977. ERIC ED156106. Microfiche.
A20

Abstract: Information is presented on the experiences, benefits, and
impact costs of the PLAN Project for public libraries in California.
System benefits and problems as related to areas in library technical
processing affected by BALLOTS are identified and discussed.

West, Martha and Brett Butler. "Performance Measures in Automated Systems
    Management." In *The Economics of Library Automation*, 1976 Clinic on
    Library Applications of Data Processing, pp. 48-71. Urbana:
    University of Illinois Graduate School of Library and Information
A21 Science, 1977.

Abstract: Discusses available techniques for performance measurement
and evaluation of automated systems and the weaknesses of these tools.
Proposed a model program of cost and task analysis and performance
measurement.

Elliott, Roger W. "Kiviat-Graphs as a Means for Displaying Performance
    Data for On-line Retrieval Systems." *Journal of the American Society*
A22 *for Information Science* 27 (May-June 1976): 178-182.

Abstract: Shows an application of the Kiviat-graph for plotting
information system performance. This technique for plotting a number
of parameters on the same axis is useful when one must keep track of a
large number of inter-related parameters.

Grosch, Audrey N. "Library Automation." *Annual Review of Information*
    Science and Technology 11 (1976): 225-266.
A23

Abstract: Review article on library automation, defined as the
application of the computer to routine operations and services in a
library. Reference is made to many technical services applications.

Hindle, Anthony and Diane Raper. "The Economics of Information." *Annual Review of Information Science and Technology* 11 (1976): 27-54.

A24

  Abstract: Review article on the economic analysis of information policy that includes some references relevant to technical services.

Montague, Eleanor and others. "Survey of Costs in Technical Processing and Interlibrary Loan: Survey Tables and Results of Case Studies." 1976. ERIC ED148359. Microfiche.

A25

  Abstract: 100 western libraries were surveyed by the Western Interstate Library Coordinating Organization to determine the present costs of library operations that potentially could be affected by the use of network bibliographic services, including acquisition and cataloging departments' budgeting, staffing, and processing patterns. Results are reported in tabular format.

Alper, Bruce H. "Library Automation." *Annual Review of Information Science and Technology* 10 (1975): 199-236.

A26

  Abstract: This review article places heavy emphasis on the examination of existing library automation systems and their performance. Some pertain to technical services.

Swanson, Rowena Weiss. "Design and Evaluation of Information Systems." *Annual Review of Information Science and Technology* 10 (1975): 43-101.

A27

  Abstract: Review article covering the period 1973-1974 includes references to numerous studies relating to the design and evaluation of information systems in technical services.

Zmud, Robert W. "Selecting Computer Resources for Inclusion within a Pricing System." *Journal of the American Society for Information Science* 26 (November-December 1975): 346-348.

A28

  Abstract: A study to discover which computer resources can be validated for inclusion within a pricing structure. Prices are seen as a means of allocating computer resources. Core space and CPU time were found to be the most suitable.

PRODUCTIVITY AND COST STATISTICS

Getz, Malcolm and Doug Phelps. "Labor Costs in the Technical Operation of Three Research Libraries." *Journal of Academic Librarianship* 10 (September 1984): 209-219.

A29

Abstract: Cost studies of technical services operations in three middle-sized research libraries. The focus of the studies was on costs of labor and the effects of automation.

Dole, Wanda V. and David Allerton. "University Collections: A Survey of Costs." *Library Acquisitions: Practice and Theory* 6 (1982): 25-32.

A30

Abstract: Report on a survey of 184 OCLC libraries to determine the costs for the acquisition and processing of materials for university collections, defined as collections composed of all book materials written by faculty, staff, and alumni as well as books about the particular institution.

Maher, William J. "Measurement and Analysis of Processing Costs in Academic Archives." *College and Research Libraries* 43 (January 1982): 59-67.

A31

Abstract: Proposes two procedures for cost studies and described the results of such studies at the University of Illinois at Urbana-Champaign. It concludes with a description of processing efficiency measurements and suggestions for the application of study findings to program operations.

Hendrickson, Leslie and Marie Celestre. "An Evaluation of an Oregon School District's Centralized Ordering and Processing System." *Library Resources and Technical Services* 25 (April/June 1981): 162-176.

A32

Abstract: This evaluation of a medium-sized school district's centralized ordering and processing system was undertaken to investigate complaints about time lags in the operation of the system. Data were collected through interviews, questionnaires, and a random sample search of ordering and processing records.

Mullikin, Angela G. "The King Research Project: Design for a Library Catalog Cost Model." *Library Resources and Technical Services* 25 (April/June 1981): 177-185.

A33

Abstract: The Association of Research Libraries sponsored the development of a library catalog cost model. The 72 participating libraries considered alternate forms of catalogs, including various combinations of card, COM, and online, in unified or split forms and prepared input data for computer runs to arrive at costs. Definite conclusions were impossible because of many variables.

Bierman, Kenneth. "Overview of the Cost of Acquiring, Cataloging, and Processing Library Materials at the Tucson Public Library." 1980. ERIC ED194089. Microfiche.

A34

Abstract: Synopsis of three studies conducted in Technical Services at the Tucson Public Library from January 1977-June 1980 showing estimated costs of acquiring, cataloging, and processing print and non-print items. Presents cost data taken from the three studies.

Mick, Colin K. "Cost analysis of Information Systems and Services." *Annual Review of Information Science and Technology* 14 (1979): 37-64.

A35

Abstract: Article reviewing representative key studies published between 1975 and 1979 dealing with cost analysis of information systems and services. A number of studies relating to the technical services are included.

Cayless, C. F. and C. G. Merritt. "The Keeping Cost of Periodicals." *Australian Academic and Research Libraries* 8 (December 1977): 178-185.

A36

Abstract: Describes a formula for determining the keeping cost of a serial title (i.e., the cost of getting it into the library and maintaining it, not including subscription cost). The eleven elements of the formula include such things as average annual fixed costs, standard unit times for procedures such as checking and binding, and salary (and overhead) costs per minute of work. The formula focuses on the cost of an individual title, so that differences in keeping cost from title to title may be shown.

McGregor, James Wilson. "Serials Staffing in Academic Libraries." <u>Serials Librarian</u> 1 (Spring 1977): 259-272.

A37

    <u>Abstract</u>: Analysis of experience and educational background of serials works, the time per title used for serials processing functions, and the number of staff needed for serials processing. Based on investigations of 48 libraries at 9 universities in 1975.

Price, Douglas S. "Cost Analysis and Reporting as a Basis for Decision." In <u>The Economics of Library Automation</u>, 1976 Clinic on Library Applications of Data Processing, pp. 83-106. Urbana: University of
A38 Illinois Graduate School of Library and Information Science, 1977.

    <u>Abstract</u>: Suggests use of "building block costing" as a method of providing library cost information useful for management decisions. Describes the elements of the method and provides some examples.

Ross, Ryburn M. "Cost Analysis of Automation in Technical Services." In <u>The Economics of Library Automation</u>, 1976 Clinic on Library Applications of Data Processing, pp. 10-27. Urbana: University of
A39 Illinois Graduate School of Library and Information Science, 1977.

    <u>Abstract</u>: Develops costs for automation activities, with specific information on cataloging costs before and after automation. Presents some information on productivity measurement and proposes techniques to measure technical services staff performance.

Southwell, T. B. "A Price-Movement Index for an Australian University Library." <u>Australian Academic and Research Libraries</u> 8 (June 1977):
A40 68-70.

    <u>Abstract</u>: Describes development of a price-movement index for mean purchase cost per item of monographs, mean subscription prices for serials, mean binding cost per periodical volume, for July 1975-March 1977 at Monash University Library.

Stewart, Blair. "The Cost of Providing Access to Periodical Literature in Academic Libraries." <u>Catholic Library World</u> 49 (September 1977): 70-
A41 75.

    <u>Abstract</u>: Discusses the use of the Associated Colleges of the Midwest Periodical Bank by its member libraries and explores the cost effectiveness of such use.

Brown, Maryann Kevin and Anita L. McHugh. "Survey of Costs in Technical Processing and Interlibrary Loan." 1976. ERIC ED148358. Microfiche.

A42

Abstract: This report, a part of the Cost and Funding Studies supportive of the development and implementation of western interstate bibliographic network capabilities, summarizes the results of cost data collected in 76 western libraries--public, academic and state. Based upon a stratified sample of 100 libraries, these studies document present costs incurred for cataloging, acquisitions, serials processing and interlibrary loan.

Montague, Eleanor and others. "Survey of Costs in Technical Processing and Interlibrary Loan: Survey Tables and Results of Case Studies." 1976.
A43   ERIC ED148359. Microfiche.

Abstract: 100 western libraries were surveyed by the Western Interstate Library Coordinating Organization to determine the present costs of library operations which potentially could be affected by the use of network bibliographic services, including acquisition and cataloging departments' budgeting, staffing, and processing patterns. Results are reported in tabular format.

Raouf, Abdul, Feroz Ahmed and Syed M. Asad. "A Performance Prediction Model for Bibliographic Search for Monographs Using Multiple Regression Technique." Journal of Library Automation 9 (September
A44   1976): 210-221.

Abstract: Uses a regression model to evaluate and control the performance of bibliographic search procedures. Also explores possibility of using the same technique in developing regression models for assessing performance of other areas.

Waldhart, Thomas J. and Thomas P. Marcum. "Productivity Measurement in Academic Libraries." Advances in Librarianship 6 (1976): 53-78.
A45

Abstract: Review article that examines productivity measurement and programs of productivity improvement in academic libraries and the relationship of increasing productivity to long-term economic stability.

West, Martha W. and Barbara A. Baxter. "Unpublished Studies of Technical
    Service Time and Costs: A Supplement." Library Resources and
A46   Technical Services 20 (Fall 1976): 326-333.

Abstract: Annotated citations report a number of productivity and cost
studies, and include a variety of cost data such as cost per title and
elapsed time per title.

CHAPTER 2

ACQUISITIONS

GENERAL AND MISCELLANEOUS

Broadus, Robert N. "A Proposed Method for Eliminating Titles from Periodical Subscription Lists." <u>College and Research Libraries</u> 46
B1 (January 1985): 30-35.

    <u>Abstract</u>: A method is outlined for determining what periodical titles should be reviewed for cancellation by a university library. A list of candidates for elimination is gathered from titles with low citation counts as found in <u>Journal Citation Reports</u>.

Line, Maurice B. "Use of Citation Data for Periodicals Control in Libraries: A Response to Broadus." <u>College and Research Libraries</u> 46
B2 (January 1985): 36-37. (With response from Broadus, p. 38-39).

    <u>Abstract</u>: Response to Broadus' article (<u>College and Research Libraries</u> 46, January 1985) on using low citation-count as a guide to journal cancellations, cautioning careful use of citation counts.

Serebnick, Judith and John Cullars. "An Analysis of Reviews and Library Holdings of Small Publishers' Books." <u>Library Resources and Technical</u>
B3 <u>Services</u> 28 (January/March 1984): 4-14.

    <u>Abstract</u>: Report on a random sample of 1980 books from <u>Small Press Record of Books in Print</u> which were searched for reviews in three indexes and in OCLC for holdings records. The findings suggest that information on the books of small publishers is more readily available than has been assumed.

Yu, Priscilla C. "National Library of China: The Acquisition of Foreign Language Materials." <u>Library Acquisitions: Practice and Theory</u> 8
B4 (1984): 1-9.

    <u>Abstract</u>: Examines the growth of the acquisition of foreign language materials in the National Library of China and the effect of historical and contemporary events on the National Library's development.

Calhoun, John and James K. Bracken. "An Index of Publisher Quality for the Academic Library." College and Research Libraries 44 (May 1983): 257-259.
B5

Abstract: Reports the construction of a publisher quality index by comparing the number of a publisher's books appearing in Choice's "Outstanding Academic Books" list with a publisher's total output.

Chudamani, K. S. and R. Shalini. "Journal Acquisition - Cost Effectiveness of Models." Information Processing and Management 19 (1983): 307-311.
B6

Abstract: Compares three different models for journal acquisitions. These models are: a. cost effectiveness, b. effectiveness and total size, and c. effectiveness and individual subscription cost. Also mentions: unit of effectiveness, method of ranking, threshold point, and graphs.

Mendenhall, Kathryn. "A Survey of the Cataloging in Publication Program. Final Report." 1982 ERIC ED221215. Microfiche.
B7

Abstract: Report of a survey of 2,366 randomly selected U. S. libraries, describing the use and impact of the CIP program. Results reveal heavy use of CIP in technical services and little use in public services. Extensive use of tables present the results of the survey.

Groot, Elizabeth H. "A Comparison of Library Tools for Monograph Verification." Library Resources and Technical Services 25 (April/June 1981): 149-161.
B8

Abstract: Six commonly used library tools were compared as to their effectiveness for verification of monographs before acquisition. A computer program was used to calculate the retrieval percentages for all possible combinations of the reference tools, over three periods of time. A cost-analysis method was developed that will permit a library of any size to determine which of the reference tools will be best for its purposes.

Hendrickson, Leslie and Marie Celestre. "An Evaluation of an Oregon School
District's Centralized Ordering and Processing System." <u>Library
Resources and Technical Services</u> 25 (April/June 1981): 162-176.

B9

<u>Abstract</u>: This evaluation of a medium-sized school district's
centralized ordering and processing system was undertaken to
investigate complaints about time lags in the operation of the system.
Data were collected through interviews, questionnaires, and a random
sample search of ordering and processing records.

Maffeo, Steven E. "Invoice Payment by Library Acquisitions: A Controlled
Time Study." <u>Library Acquisitions: Practice and Theory</u> 5 (1981):
67-71.

B10

<u>Abstract</u>: Statistical examination of time spans elapsing between
monitorable accounts payable functions within a library acquisitions
context. The derivatives were computed providing specific,
quantitative system analysis for internal accountability.

Bierman, Kenneth J. and others. "Unit Time/Cost Study of the Acquisitions
Unit, Technical Services Division, Tucson Public Library." 1980.
ERIC ED194090. Microfiche.

B11

<u>Abstract</u>: Report of the third and final Technical Services study
designed to develop unit time and costs for the major operations of
the Acquisitions Unit (excluding selection).

Erlandson, John and Yvonne Boyer. "Acquisition of State Documents."
<u>Library Acquisitions: Practice and Theory</u> 4 (1980): 117-127.

B12

<u>Abstract</u>: Study of the acquisition of state document materials based
on individual selection sources used. Sources covered in the study
include <u>Monthly Checklist of State Publications, PAIS</u>, LC cards, and
various state checklists.

Jarmy, Imre T. "1978 Library Microfilm Rates." <u>Library Resources and
Technical Services</u> 24 (Spring 1980): 164-169.

B13

<u>Abstract</u>: An analysis of rates charged by selected U. S. libraries
for producing 35mm, archival quality, silver halide microfilm, with
tentative projections of future rates based on current market
conditions.

Law, Derek G. "Acquisitions and their Processing in Edinburg University Library: Results of a Survey." Aslib Proceedings 32 (November/December 1980): 459-467.

B14

Abstract: Survey of acquisitions processes over a three month time period. Acquisitions are analyzed by country, language, and date of publication. The time taken to acquire the publications is also measured. Article concentrates on Scotland and university libraries.

Cohen, Jacob and Kenneth W. Leeson. "Sources and Uses of Funds of Academic Libraries." Library Trends 28 (Summer 1979): 25-46.

B15

Abstract: Analysis of where university libraries obtain their money and how they spend it based primarily on two studies: Machlup and Leeson on the uses of funds and ARL on the sources of funds.

Maher, William J. and Benjamin F. Shearer. "Undergraduate Use Patterns of Newspapers on Microfilm." College and Research Libraries 40 (May 1979): 254-260.

B16

Abstract: This analysis, based on undergraduate use patterns of newspapers on microfilm at the University of Illinois, presents criteria, such as number of titles, dates requested, and existence of indexes, that should be considered when purchasing microfilmed newspapers.

Wenger, Charles B., Christine B. Sweet and Helen J. Stiles. "Monograph Evaluation for Acquisitions in a Large Research Library." Journal of the American Society for Information Science 30 (March 1979): 88-92.

B17

Abstract: Presents a computerized method of assisting monograph collection development by correlating circulation with inventory statistics. A circulation/inventory/time or circulation/inventory/ ratio is used to identify high and low use subject areas. The data can then be used to determine areas in which more or fewer purchases should be made.

Flowers, Janet L. "Time Logs for Searchers: How Useful?" Library Acquisitions: Practice and Theory 2 (1978): 77-83.

B18

Abstract: A study of the operations of the pre-order searching unit at a major university library through the use of time logs.

Hodowanec, George V. "An Acquisition Rate Model for Academic Libraries." <u>College and Research Libraries</u> 39 (November 1978): 439-447.
B19

<u>Abstract</u>: With circulation assumed to imply use and thus need, multiple regression analysis was employed to determine which variables best correlate with circulation. A regression equation recommending a predictive value for the number of books to be added was developed.

Lincoln, Robert. "Controlling Duplicate Orders or, Riding A Camel." <u>Library Acquisitions: Practice and Theory</u> 2 (1978): 143-150.
B20

<u>Abstract</u>: A discussion of the duplicate order control system at a university library aimed at the reduction of purchasing unwanted duplicates.

Broadus, Robert N. "The Applications of Citation Analysis to Library Collection Building." <u>Advances in Librarianship</u> 7 (1977): 299-335.
B21

<u>Abstract</u>: Review article on citation studies for use in the selection process. Citation studies are seen as holding some hope for the improvement of the quality of selection.

Clement, Russell T. "The Duplicate-Replacement System: An Alternative Method of Handling Book Duplicates." 1977. ERIC ED152308.
B22 Microfiche.

<u>Abstract</u>: This report studied the alternative method of using book duplicates as replacement copies for worn or missing stack items. When tested in the Brigham Young University's Lee Library, it cost an estimated $110 and saved over $4,000 for the replacement of 1,000 books.

Lupton, David Walker. "Serials Subscription Payment Losses; An Analysis." <u>Library Acquisitions: Practice and Theory</u> 1 (January 1977): 3-6.
B23

<u>Abstract</u>: A study of serials payment records from a medium-sized academic library over a nineteen-year period to identify sources of losses and to remind library staff that reviews of payment records are necessary to monitoring and control.

Reid, Marion T. "Effectiveness of the OCLC Data Base for Acquisitions Verification." <u>Journal of Academic Librarianship</u> 2 (January 1977): 303-326.

B24

<u>Abstract</u>: A study to evaluate the effectiveness of the OCLC database as an acquisitions verification tool in comparison to conventional library search tools.

Saracevic, T., W.M. Shaw, Jr. and P.B. Kantor. "Causes and Dynamics of User Frustration in an Academic Library." <u>College and Research Libraries</u> 38 (January 1977): 7-18.

B25

<u>Abstract</u>: A method of analysis was developed that allows for the calculation of four independent probabilities indicating measures of performance of acquisitions policy, circulation policy, library operations, and users. It is argued that the branching analysis for the combination of effects and the particular measures derived are universally applicable for studying these aspects of library performance.

Brown, Maryann Kevin and Anita L. McHugh. "Survey of Costs in Technical Processing and Interlibrary Loan." 1976. ERIC ED148358. Microfiche.

B26

<u>Abstract</u>: This report, a part of the Cost and Funding Studies supportive of the development and implementation of western interstate bibliographic network capabilities, summarizes the results of cost data collected in 76 western libraries--public, academic and state. Based upon a stratified sample of 100 libraries, these studies document present costs incurred for cataloging, acquisitions, serials processing and interlibrary loan.

Cushman, Ruth Carol. "Lease Plans--A New Lease on Life for Libraries?" <u>Journal of Academic Librarianship</u> 2 (March 1976): 15-19.

B27

<u>Abstract</u>: Results of a survey to determine the use of book lease plans in academic libraries and their attendant advantages and disadvantages.

Huff, William H. "Serial Subscription Agencies." <u>Library Trends</u> 24 (April 1976): 683-709).

B28

<u>Abstract</u>: A discussion of the serial subscription agency and its relationship to libraries. Included is a section on costs.

Raouf, Abdul, Feroz Ahmed and Syed M. Asad. "A Performance Prediction Model for Bibliographic Search for Monographs Using Multiple Regression Technique." *Journal of Library Automation* 9 (September 1976): 210-221.

B29

    Abstract: Uses a regression model to evaluate and control the performance of bibliographic search procedures. Also explores possibility of using the same technique in developing regression models for assessing performance of other areas.

DePew, John N. "An Acquisitions Decision Model for Academic Libraries." *Journal of the American Society for Information Science* 26 (July-August 1975): 237-246.

B30

    Abstract: Describes a tentative decision model for book acquisitions that includes weighted inputs and an equation to indicate whether a library should add a title to its collection, refer it to a cooperative group, defer decision, or drop consideration of the title.

Kosa, Geza A. "Book Selection Tools for Subject Specialists in a Large Research Library: An Analysis." *Library Resources and Technical Services* 19 (Winter 1975): 13-18.

B31

    Abstract: Order slips were analyzed to determine the relative usefulness to subject specialists of various selection aids. The two most useful types of sources for selection were bibliographies and publisher's advertisements.

APPROVAL PLANS

Reidelbach, John H. and Gary M. Shirk. "Selecting an Approval Plan Vendor III: Academic Librarians' Evaluations of Eight United States Approval Plan Vendors." *Library Acquisitions: Practice and Theory* 9 (1985): 177-260.

B32

    Abstract: The third of three articles concerning the evaluation and selection of an approval plan vendor for a college or university library. Experiences of more than 100 academic librarians with one or more of eight U. S. approval plan vendors are reported.

Reidelbach, John H. and Gary M. Shirk. "Selecting an Approval Plan Vendor II: Comparative Vendor Data." *Library Acquisitions: Practice and Theory* 8 (1984): 157-202.

B33

Abstract: The second of three articles intended to reduce the time, cost and risk of selecting a domestic approval plan vendor for a college or university library. Comparison of data collected from eight major U. S. approval plan vendors covering: company background, employee background, customer service, profile and title selection, profile maintenance, material forms/slips/returns handling, financial practices, statistical reporting, and miscellaneous data.

Dole, Wanda V. "Austerity and the Arts: Collection Development in the 1980's." *Drexel Library Quarterly* 19 (Summer 1983): 28-37.

B34

Abstract: As one type of currently available tool for collection development, describes a cost and coverage study of fine arts titles treated on the approval plans of two vendors.

Perrault, Anna H. "A New Dimension in Approval Plan Service." *Library Acquisitions: Practice and Theory* 7 (1983): 35-40.

B35

Abstract: Presents results of a three-month study conducted using the fiche database service offered by a major approval plan vendor and three review tools. The object of the study was to assess the utility of the fiche service to a selector for determining the status of new publications with respect to the library approval program at the time of review. A secondary objective was to assess the usefulness of the fiche service as a tool for monitoring the effectiveness of the vendor's interpretation and implementation of a library's approval plan service.

Reidelbach, John H. and Gary M. Shirk. "Selecting an Approval Plan Vendor: A Step-By-Step Process." *Library Acquisitions: Practice and Theory* 7 (1983): 115-122.

B36

Abstract: Describes a practical process for use in evaluating and selecting a domestic approval plan vendor once the decision to use a plan has been made. Details 10 steps including the establishment of preliminary approval plan design, verification of current vendor performance at other comparable academic libraries and notification of the selected vendor.

Leonhart, Thomas W. "Approval Plans in ARL Libraries. SPEC Kit 83."
1982. ERIC ED220100. Microfiche.
B37

Abstract: Report of a survey of ARL libraries on the numbers and types of approval plans in use. In addition to a tally of responses, extensive appendices include analyses and statistical tables on approval plan acquisitions, performance, and evaluation from several respondents.

Gregor, Jan and Wendy Carol Fraser. "A University of Windsor Experience with an Approval Plan in Three Subjects and Three Vendors."
B38 Canadian Library Journal 38 (August 1981): 227-231.

Abstract: Analysis of approval plan vendor performance using the criteria of delivery time, comprehensive subject coverage, and price.

Newborn, Dennis E. and Irene P. Godden. "Approval Plan Performance: A Case Study." Library Acquisitions: Practice and Theory 4 (1980):
B39 145-155.

Abstract: A study to compare unit costs per approval plan title acquired based on two different systems of internal procedures.

McDonald, David R., Margaret W. Maxfield and Virginia G. F. Friesner. "Sequential Analysis: a Methodology for Monitoring Approval Plans."
B40 College and Research Libraries 40 (July 1979): 329-334.

Abstract: Sequential analysis, a statistical method based on drawing sample items one at a time, is applied to investigating the performance of a library approval plan. Application of the methodology at an academic library is reported in detail, and adaptations to other library situations are explained.

Grand, Joan and Susan Perelmuter. "Vendor Performance Evaluation." Journal of Academic Librarianship 4 (1978): 366-367.
B41

Abstract: Analysis of three approval plan vendors by comparing speed, bibliographic accuracy, and discounts.

Hulbert, Linda Ann and David Stewart Curry. "Evaluation of an Approval Plan." College and Research Libraries 39 (November 1978): 485-491.
B42

Abstract: Results of a study evaluating an approval plan employed by a health sciences library are reported.

Axford, William H. "The Validity of Book Price Indexes for Budgetary Projections." *Library Resources and Technical Services* 19 (Winter 1975): 5-12.

B43

> Abstract: A comparison of the average prices paid for books received through approval plans and the average prices listed annually in the *Bowker Annual*. Results indicate that the average price paid per title through approval plans is a more reliable guide for budgetary projections than the average price per volume of titles listed in the trade sources.

DeVilbiss, Mary Lee. "The Approval-Built Collection in the Medium-Sized Academic Library." *College and Research Libraries* 36 (November 1975): 487-492.

B44

> Abstract: The study compares the approval-built collection with the collection that is created when traditional selection and order procedures are used. The study was limited to 1974 imprints in four subject areas and utilized the services of two major vendors.

McCullough, Kathleen. "Approval Plans and Departmental Fair Share." (April 1975) ERIC ED111340. Microfiche.

B45

> Abstract: Analyzes approval plan receipts and selections by subject and compares them to proportions of books by subject in general publishing. Results indicate that approval plan selections parallel subject proportions in general publishing.

AUTOMATION

Baldwin, Paul E. "Planning the Implementation of an Integrated On-line Acquisition System." *Canadian Library Journal* 41 (February 1984): 31-36.

B46

> Abstract: Analyzes the use of cost data to present to library management to justify implementation planning for an integrated, online acquisitions and fund accounting system.

Lundeen, Gerald W. and Charles H. Davis. "Library Automation." *Annual Review of Information Science and Technology* 17 (1982): 161-186.

B47

> Abstract: Review article covering the years 1980-1981 which looks at library automation. Sections on the technical services are included.

Miller, Bruce C. "Placing and Tracing Orders in a Dynamic Acquisitions
    Process." *Collection Management* 3 (Summer/Fall 1979): 233-246.
B48

    Abstract: Details a description of a relatively simple computer
system that provides monthly data from the entire file of outstanding
orders concerning rates of return and performance curves. The system
answers questions such as:
-how long should it take to buy a book?
-are our sources efficient and reliable?
-how much time should we spend claiming?
-when should we consider an order "dead"?
-are our outgoing orders bibliographically clear enough to insure a
healthy fulfillment rate?

Grosch, Audrey N. "Library Automation." *Annual Review of Information
    Science and Technology* 11 (1976): 225-266.
B49

    Abstract: Review article on library automation, defined as the
application of the computer to routine operations and services in a
library. Reference is made to many technical services applications.

GIFTS AND EXCHANGES

Diodato, Louise W. and Virgil P. Diodato. "The Use of Gifts in a Medium
    Sized Academic Library." *Collection Management* 5 (Spring/Summer
B50 1983): 53-69.

    Abstract: Describes two methods of evaluating gifts program. The
first model deals with the cost effectiveness of gifts and the second
assumes that if a book is used once it was worth adding to the
collection. Additional factors considered are: multiple copies and
time lag from printing to donating of gift books.

Lavigne, Jonathan. "Duplicate Exchange Lists: A Study of Costs and
    Response Patterns." *Library Acquisitions: Practice and Theory* 7
B51 (1983): 195-202.

    Abstract: Analyzes the time and costs involved in producing and
processing lists of duplicates used for exchange; gives data on
responses received from different areas around the world; surveys the
popularity of different kinds of books used; and assesses the
importance of such lists in maintaining balanced exchanges. It is
based on data gathered over a six-month period for lists issued by the
Stanford University Libraries.

Stevens, Jana K., Jade G. Kelley and Richard G. Irons. "Cost-Effectiveness of Soviet Serial Exchanges." *Library Resources and Technical Services* 26 (April/June 1982): 151-155.

B52

Abstract: A review of 26 Soviet institutions and 70 Soviet serial publications showed that the availability of Soviet publications through normal trade channels has increased in recent years.

Yu, Priscilla C. "International Gift & Exchange: The Asian Experience." *Journal of Academic Librarianship* 6 (January 1981): 333-338.

B53

Abstract: Study of common patterns and problems relating to gift and exchange programs of American academic and research libraries.

Kovacic, Mark. "Gifts and Exchanges in U. S. Academic Libraries." *Library Resources and Technical Services* 24 (Spring 1980): 155-163.

B54

Abstract: Visits to libraries to study their gift and exchange programs result in information about policies and procedures, and organization and staffing of gift and exchange programs.

Ejlerson, Rita. "The Economic Aspect of the Exchange of Duplicates: Time Studies on Books; A Case Study." 1979. ERIC ED185997. Microfiche.

B55

Abstract: Report of a ten-month study performed at the Institut Danois des Exchanges Internationaux de Publications Scientifiques et Litteraires (IDE) on its exchange program for duplicate monographs which provides an analysis of the working methods and time spent on the various phases, i.e., acquisition, processing, and distribution.

Einhorn, Nathan R. "The Inclusion of the Products of Reprography in the International Exchange of Publications." *Library Acquisitions: Practice and Theory* 1 (1978): 227-236.

B56

Abstract: A study of the use of reprographic materials in the international exchange of publications.

Eggleton, Richard. "The ALA Duplicates Exchange Union--a Study and Evaluation." *Library Resources and Technical Services* 19 (Spring 1975): 148-163.

B57

Abstract: A questionnaire was sent to all Duplicates Exchange Union members, dealing with all aspects of DEU operations. The analysis of responses highlights problems in the structure and operation of the union.

Skelley, Grant T. "Characteristics of Collections Added to American Research Libraries, 1940-1970: A Preliminary Investigation."
B58 *College and Research Libraries* 36 (January 1975): 52-60.

Abstract: During the years 1940-1970 301 American libraries were reported in *College and Research Libraries* and *College and Research Libraries News* to have added 1454 collections. In this report the collections are analyzed by (1) type of library, (2) type of collection, (3) means acquired, and (4) sources of gifts to academic libraries.

MATERIALS BUDGET

Bently, Stella and David Farrell. "Beyond Retrenchment: The Reallocation of a Library Materials Budget." *Journal of Academic Librarianship* 10
B59 (January 1985): 321-325.

Abstract: A study of the materials budget allocation procedure at a large research library in conjunction with a survey of peer institutions.

Emery, Charles D. "Forecasting Models and the Prediction of Periodical Subscription Costs." *Serials Librarian* 9 (Summer 1985): 5-22.
B60
Abstract: Suggests models that may be used to predict periodical subscription costs and proposes guidelines for designing and implementing a forecasting system. Several selected forecasting models were tested against a time-series of periodical prices, using the mean average deviation as the comparison; the model based on the geometric mean proved most reliable.

Horn, Judith G. and Rebecca T. Lenzini. "Price Indexes for 1985: U. S. Periodicals." *Library Journal* 110 (August 1985): 53-58.
B61
Abstract: Continuation of annual study of American periodical prices by subject area. Previously compiled by Norman Brown and Jane Phillips.

Joyce, Patrick and Thomas E. Merz. "Price Discrimination in Academic Journals." <u>Library Quarterly</u> 55 (July 1985): 273-283.

B62

    <u>Abstract</u>: Analysis of price discrimination, the practice of charging different prices to different customers for the same product, for 89 academic journals. Subject areas covered include chemistry, physics, psychology, economics, sociology, and business.

Lenzini, Rebecca T. "Periodical Prices 1983-1985 Update." <u>Serials Librarian</u> 9 (Summer 1985): 119-130.

B63

    <u>Abstract</u>: Reports Faxon's 3 year comparative price studies for 1983, 1984 and 1985, with tables and charts similar to previous years.

Messineo, Leonard. Supply-Side Measurement: A Formulation for the Allocation of Book Funds in Public Libraries." <u>Technical Services Quarterly</u> 2 (Spring/Summer 1985): 61-72.

B64

    <u>Abstract</u>: Discusses the advantages of allocating the public library book budget according to the price factored book title output of the book industry.

Ruschin, Siegfried. "Why are Foreign Subscription Rates Higher for American Libraries Than They are for Subscribers Elsewhere?" <u>Serials Librarian</u> 9 (Spring 1985): 7-17.

B65

    <u>Abstract</u>: Compares subscription rates for North American subscribers to those charged British, European and other subscribers.

Brown, Norman B. and Jane Phillips. "Price Indexes for 1984: U. S. Periodicals and Serial Services." <u>Library Journal</u> 109 (August 1984): 1422-1425.

-----. "Price Indexes for 1983: U. S. Periodicals and Serial Services." <u>Library Journal</u> 108 (September 1, 1983): 1659-1662.

-----. "Price Indexes for 1982: U. S. Periodicals and Serial Services." <u>Library Journal</u> 107 (August 1982): 1379-1382.

-----. "Price Indexes for 1981: U. S. Periodicals and Serial Services." <u>Library Journal</u> 106 (July 1981): 1387-1393.

-----. "Price Indexes for 1980: U. S. Periodicals and Serial Services." <u>Library Journal</u> 105 (July 1980): 1486-1491.

-----. "Price Indexes for 1979: U. S. Periodicals and Serial Services." <u>Library Journal</u> 104 (September 1, 1979): 1628-1633.

Brown, Norman B. "Price Indexes for 1978: U. S. Periodicals and Serial Services." <u>Library Journal</u> 103 (July 1978): 1356-1361.
-----. "Price Indexes for 1977: U. S. Periodicals and Serial Services." <u>Library Journal</u> 102 (July 1977): 1462-1467.
-----. "Price Indexes for 1976: U. S. Periodicals and Serial Services." <u>Library Journal</u> 101 (August 1976): 1600-1605.
-----. "Price Indexes for 1975: U. S. Periodicals and Serial Services." <u>Library Journal</u> 100 (July 1975): 1291-1295.

B66

<u>Abstract</u>: Annual study of the cost of American periodicals and serial services by subject area. Continued for 1985 by Judith G. Horn and Rebecca T. Lenzini.

Hamaker, Charles and Deana Astle. "Recent Pricing Patterns in British Journal Publishing." <u>Library Acquisitions: Practice and Theory</u> 8
B67 (1984): 225-232.

<u>Abstract</u>: A study of the 1984 price lists of seventeen British journal publishers to determine pricing patterns for subscriptions sent to American libraries.

Lenzini, Rebecca T. "Periodical Prices 1982-1984 Update." <u>Serials Librarian</u> 9 (Winter 1984): 13-24.
B68

<u>Abstract</u>: Reports the 3 year comparative price studies for 1982, 1983 and 1984 compiled by the Faxon Company. The tables and analytical charts are generally similar to those presented earlier. The 1984 data are based on 9 rather than 12 months due to a change in Faxon's fiscal year.

Schmitz-Veltin, Gerhard and John J. Boll. "Literature Use as a Measure for Funds Allocation." <u>Library Acquisitions: Practice and Theory</u> 8
B69 (1984): 267-274.

<u>Abstract</u>: Discussion of a technique developed by the University of Constance in West Germany for using past circulation figures as a major factor in allocating the monographic acquisitions budget among various subjects. Additional factors covered include the proportionate purchases made in each subject field during the preceding three years and the price per volume in each subject field. Originally published in <u>Zeitschrift fur Bibliothekswesen und Bibliographie</u> 31 (January/February 1984): 9-17.

Smith, Dennis. "Forecasting Price Increase Needs for Library Materials: The University of California Experience." <u>Library Resources and Technical Services</u> 28 (April/June 1984): 136-148.

B70

    <u>Abstract</u>: Discusses plans to establish an adequate base book budget and to measure price increase needs to maintain budgeted acquisition rates. The plan also seeks to maintain book budget increases and a balanced budget acquisition rate among the campuses.

Alison, Jennifer. "Recent Australian Serial Prices." <u>Australian Academic and Research Libraries</u> 14 (March 1983): 55-58.

B71

    <u>Abstract</u>: Compares average serial prices in 1971, 1975, and 1981, using data from <u>Current Australian Serials</u> and <u>Australian Serials in Print</u>. Gives breakdown by subject for price changes between 1975 and 1981.

Dyl, Edward A. "A Note on Price Discrimination by Academic Journals." <u>Library Quarterly</u> 53 (April 1983): 161-168.

B72

    <u>Abstract</u>: Comparative study of prices of academic journals for libraries and for individual subscribers.

Holland, Maurita Peterson. "Machine-Readable Files for Serials Management: an Optimizing Program and Use Data." <u>College and Research Libraries</u> 44 (January 1983): 66-69.

B73

    <u>Abstract</u>: The files of data created to support use of a formula to assess serial "value" (reported in <u>College and Research Libraries</u> 37, November 1976) are applied to other kinds of objective serials budget analyses.

Lenzini, Rebecca T. "Periodical Prices 1981-1983 Update." <u>Serials Librarian</u> 8 (Winter 1983): 107-118.

B74

    <u>Abstract</u>: Continues the 3 year comparative periodical price studies completed earlier by F. F. Clasquin and Gerald R. Lowell of F. W. Faxon Company. A variety of tables and comparative information is presented.

Lynden, Frederick C. "Library Material Cost Studies." <u>Library Resources and Technical Services</u> 27 (April/June 1983): 156-162.

B75

<u>Abstract</u>: Describes the need for cost data, and the general lack of cost data or a regular communication system for such data. Discusses compilation techniques.

McPheron, William. "Quantifying the Allocation of Monograph Funds: An Instance in Practice." <u>College and Research Libraries</u> 44 (March 1983): 116-127.

B76

<u>Abstract</u>: This paper describes a formula for distributing monograph funds that employs a size-of-literature approach to the allocations process but significantly alters traditional versions of that model.

Dole, Wanda V. and David Allerton. "University Collections: A Survey of Costs." <u>Library Acquisitions: Practice and Theory</u> 6 (1982): 25-32.

B77

<u>Abstract</u>: Report on a survey of 184 OCLC libraries to determine the costs for acquisition and processing of materials for university collections, defined as collections composed of all book materials written by faculty, staff, and alumni as well as books about the particular institution.

Gleaves, Edwin S. and Robert T. Carterette. "Microform Serials Acquisition: A Suggested Planning Model." <u>Journal of Academic Librarianship</u> 8 (November 1982): 292-295.

B78

<u>Abstract</u>: A model for estimating expected costs and savings from a microform serials acquisitions program.

Lowell, Gerald R. "Periodical Prices 1980-1982 Update." <u>Serials Librarian</u> 7 (Fall 1982): 75-83.

B79

<u>Abstract</u>: An annual update to the 3-year price reviews published by Faxon since 1974; previous updates were published in <u>Library Journal</u> and <u>Serials Librarian</u>. Prices increased an average of 18.5% in 1981 and 9% in 1982.

Belanger, Charles H. and Lise Lavallee. "Towards a Periodical and Monograph Price Index." <u>College and Research Libraries</u> 42 (September 1981): 416-424.

B80

    <u>Abstract</u>: Examines the various steps and intricacies involved in tailoring a periodical and monograph price index to a university library and looks at a number of issues librarians are wrestling with in an attempt to balance their acquisition budgets.

Ching-Tat, Lee. "Acquisitions Budget Control in a CAE Library." <u>Australian Academic and Research Libraries</u> 12 (September 1981): 174-184.

B81

    <u>Abstract</u>: Presents a formula for distributing book acquisition funds by subject in terms of course areas, student and staff numbers, and average cost per volume. Applies the formula in a technical college library.

Clasquin, F. F. "The 1978-80 Faxon Periodical Prices Update." <u>Serials Librarian</u> 5 (Spring 1981): 81-90.

B82

    <u>Abstract</u>: Presents average prices and price increases by subject for the 3 year period, 1978 through 1980.

Kronenfeld, Michael R. and James A. Thompson. "The Impact of Inflation on Journal Costs." <u>Library Journal</u> 106 (April 1, 1981): 714-717.

B83

    <u>Abstract</u>: Analysis to determine whether or not journal prices rose at a more rapid rate than inflation.

Lowell, Gerald R. "Periodical Prices 1978-1981 Update." <u>Serials Librarian</u> 5 (Spring 1981): 91-99.

B84

    <u>Abstract</u>: Continues earlier comparative price studies published by F. F. Clasquin: includes a variety of tables and analytical charts.

Strazdon, Maureen E. "A Library Application of the Apple VisiCalc Program." <u>Drexel Library Quarterly</u> 17 (Winter 1981): 75-86.

B85

    <u>Abstract</u>: Brief description of the use of VisiCalc to maintain and manipulate library collection statistics and budget information in a small library.

Walch, David B. "Price Index for Nonprint Media." <u>Library Journal</u> 106 (February 15, 1981): 432-433.

B86

    <u>Abstract</u>: Analysis of nonprint media prices to show average unit costs and cost trends for the most popular forms of media acquired by libraries.

Werking, Richard Hume and Charles S. M. Getchell, Jr. "Using <u>Choice</u> as a Mechanism for Allocating Book Funds in an Academic Library." <u>College and Research Libraries</u> 42 (March 1981): 134-138.

B87

    <u>Abstract</u>: This article reiterates the need for a "literature-size" approach to book fund allocations and presents a case for using reviews from <u>Choice</u> magazine as a useful and hitherto ignored means of determining literature size. Data from one calendar year show the number and percentages of titles and the dollar amount and percentage represented by each subject category.

Clasquin, F. F. and Jackson B. Cohen. "Biochemistry and Molecular Biology Journal Prices." <u>Serials Librarian</u> 4 (Summer 1980): 381-392.

B88

    <u>Abstract</u>: Study of biochemistry and molecular biology journal prices, 1967-1979; demonstrates how these compare in cost to physics and chemistry journals, previously found most costly. A small number of highly cited titles account for nearly 50% of the cost of the entire list of 83 journals studied.

Hentschke, Guilbert C. and Ellen Kehoe. "Serial Acquisition as a Capital Budgeting Problem." <u>Journal of the American Society for Information Science</u> 31 (September 1980): 357-362.

B89

    <u>Abstract</u>: Examines costs and benefits of purchasing periodicals on a 1-year versus a 3-year subscription basis--viewed as a capital budgeting problem extending over a six year time span. Critical variables include: cost of capital, subscription reorder costs, annual rate of change of subscription rates and ratio of 1-year to 3-year subscription costs. A model is developed.

Lynden, Frederick C. "Library Materials Budgeting in the Private University Library: Austerity and Action." <u>Advances in Librarianship</u> 10 (1980): 89-154.

B90

    <u>Abstract</u>: Review article on budgeting processes for library materials and a detailed analysis of the library materials budgeting process in 12 large private libraries. The analysis is summarized.

Sweetman, Peter and Paul Wiedemann. "Developing a Library Book-Fund Allocation Formula." *Journal of Academic Librarianship* 6 (November 1980): 268-276.

B91

Abstract: The development of a formula for allocating a library book fund is detailed along with suggested solutions to a number of practical problems in selecting a multiple-criteria allocation formula.

White, Herbert S. "Factors in the Decision by Individuals and Libraries to Place or Cancel Subscriptions to Scholarly and Research Journals." *Library Quarterly* 50 (July 1980): 287-309.

B92

Abstract: Describes a survey to gather information on the factors which prompted both individuals and libraries to place new subscriptions or cancel existing subscriptions to established scholarly and research journals.

Yunker, James A. and Carol G. Covey. "An Optimizing Approach to the Problem of Interdepartmental Allocation of the Library Materials Budget." *Library Acquisitions: Practice and Theory* 4 (1980): 199-223.

B93

Abstract: Presents a formal, mathematically expressed hypothesis concerning the effect of library spending by department on patron welfare. It then derives a formula as the solution to the problem of maximizing patron welfare within the budget constraint that the sum of the allocations to the departments must equal the total funds available.

Borlase, Rod. "A Nonlinear, Bimodal Model for Monitoring the Flow of Materials Fund Allocations (Treated as Nonmathematically as Possible)." *Journal of Academic Librarianship* 5 (November 1979): 274-276.

B94

Abstract: Describes a model for monitoring the expenditure of materials funds based on a bimodal purchasing pattern.

Clasquin, F. F. "Periodicals Prices: 1977-79 Update." *Library Journal* 104 (October 15, 1979): 2168-2171.
-----. "Periodicals Prices: 1976-78 Update." *Library Journal* 103 (October 1, 1978): 1924-1927.
-----. "Periodicals Prices: 1975-77 Update." *Library Journal* 102 (October 1, 1977): 2011-2015.
-----. "Periodicals Prices: 74-76 Update." *Library Journal* 101 (October 1, 1976): 2015-2019.
-----. "Periodicals Prices: A 1975 Update." *Library Journal* 100 (October 1, 1975): 1775-1777.

B95

Abstract: Annual comparative study of periodical prices by subject area.

Clasquin, F. F. "Physics and Chemistry Journal Prices in 1977-1978." *Serials Librarian* 3 (Summer 1979): 381-385.

B96

Abstract: Documents the continued double digit inflation for the period 1977 and 1978 for physics and chemistry journals, an extension of the subscription rate increases previously reported for the years 1973 through 1976.

Fry, Bernard M. and Herbert S. White. "Impact of Economic Pressures on American Libraries and Their Decisions Concerning Scholarly and Research Journal Acquisition and Retention." *Library Acquisitions: Practice and Theory* 3 (1979): 153-237.

B97

Abstract: Survey of economic conditions, budgetary pressures, economic alternatives, behavioral patterns, and actions and perceptions by both librarians and various publisher groups for the years 1974 and 1976. This is an update to the authors' *Publishers and Libraries: A Study of Scholarly and Research Journals*.

"The Library Dollar." *Australian Academic and Research Libraries* 10 (June 1979): 99-104.

B98

Abstract: Discusses projections for purchasing power of two Australian university libraries in 1978-1985, given expected rates of increase in book and serial prices and in library funding.

Snoball, George J. and Martin S. Cohen. "Control of Book Fund Expenditures Under an Accrual Accounting System." <u>Collection Management</u> 3 (Spring 1979): 5-20.

B99

<u>Abstract</u>: Accrual accounting (funds are considered expended at the time of encumbrance irrespective of when invoices are paid) is an attempt to control expenditures so that work flows smoothly through the acquisitions department and funds do not lapse because they have not actually been disbursed. This system is also dependent upon average book prices, volumes ordered, and a monitoring committee to ensure the smooth working of this system.

Steinbrenner, Julie. "Cost-Effectiveness of Book Rental Plans." <u>Ohio Library Association Bulletin</u> 42 (April 1979): 5-6.

B100

<u>Abstract</u>: Describes a comparison of the cost of renting and purchasing books through the McNaughton plan with the cost of purchasing the same books through Bro-Dart, Inc. at Sandusky Public Library.

Warner, Edward S. and Anita L. Anker. "Utilizing Library Constituents Perceived Needs in Allocating Journal Costs." <u>Journal of the American Society for Information Science</u> 30 (November 1979): 325-329.

B101

<u>Abstract</u>: Advocates using constituents perceived needs for titles as a means of ascribing journal collection costs to academic programs, rather than simply using the classification of journals. This also provides more realistic lists of titles in support of a particular academic program.

Clasquin, Frank F. "Financial Management of Serials and Journals Through Subject 'Core' Lists." <u>Serials Librarian</u> 2 (Spring 1978): 287-297.

B102

<u>Abstract</u>: Describes the use of the core list idea for evaluating serials collections and for preparing serials budgets. Comments on the way core lists are constructed and provides examples in the medical field.

Heroux, Marlene and Carol Fleishauer. "Cancellation Decisions: Evaluating Standing Orders." <u>Library Resources and Technical Services</u> 22 (Fall 1978): 368-379.

B103

<u>Abstract</u>: Describes a methodology for a review of standing orders in the form of a point system that rates titles according to: support of university programs, interlibrary loan availability, language, price, frequency, access by analytics, indexes or abstracts, and circulation. The system is applied to a sample of 109 titles.

Kriz, Harry M. "Subscriptions vs. Books in a Constant Dollar Budget." *College and Research Libraries* 39 (March 1978): 105-109.

B104

    Abstract: Citation analysis was used as an aid in collection development in the field of engineering, to compare the relative usefulness of journals and books to graduate students.

Pierce, Thomas J. "An Empirical Approach to the Allocation of the University Library Book Budget." *Collection Management* 2 (Spring 1978): 39-58.

B105

    Abstract: Description of the application of a statistical formula for the allocation of a university book budget. The intent of this paper is to develop an empirically based, statistical formula capable of furnishing a set of allocation figures which might aid library administrators in distributing the book budget among the departments.

Sampson, Gary S. "Allocating the Book Budget: Measuring for Inflation." *College and Research Libraries* 39 (September 1978): 381-383.

B106

    Abstract: A simple algebraic method of compensating for inflation while allocating the book budget by funds is presented. Also described are the results of attempts to generate library-resource unit cost figures based on internal measurement of buying patterns.

Sauer, Tim. "Predicting Book Fund Expenditures: A Statistical Model." *College and Research Libraries* 39 (November 1978): 474-478.

B107

    Abstract: A statistical model is developed to predict, at any point in the fiscal year, the amount of money that will be spent, within a book acquisition system, on firm orders against a given fund and thereby predict the number of orders that must still be placed in order to totally spend but not overspend that fund.

Waltner, Nellie L., Cyrus B. King and William C. Horner. "Periodical Prices: A Comparison of Local and National Averages." *Library Acquisitions: Practice and Theory* 1 (1978): 237-241.

B108

    Abstract: A study of average costs for a university library's periodicals in selected Library of Congress classification categories purchased from two major subscription agents.

Wyllys, Ronald E. "On the Analysis of Growth Rates of Library Collections and Expenditures." Collection Management 2 (Summer 1978): 115-128.
B109

    Abstract: Discusses a method of determining the average growth rate of a typical library collection. Expenditures also tend to grow exponentially; therefore, analysis of their growth rates is complicated by the effects of inflation. Different methods of compensating for inflation in the analysis are presented.

DeGennaro, Richard. "Escalating Journal Prices: Time to Fight Back. American Libraries 8 (February 1977): 69-74.
B110

    Abstract: Addresses the ever increasing costs of journals and serials in libraries. Discusses quantitative techniques for managing journal collections as well as ways to cut journal costs.

Southwell, T. B. "A Price-Movement Index for an Australian University Library." Australian Academic and Research Libraries 8 (June 1977):
B111 68-70.

    Abstract: Describes development of a price-movement index for mean purchase cost per item of monographs, mean subscription prices for serials, mean binding cost per periodical volume, for July 1975-March 1977 at Monash University Library.

Wainwright, Eric. "Letter to the Editor." Australian Academic and Research Libraries 8 (December 1977): 204-205.
B112

    Abstract: Letter about T. B. Southwell's "Price-Movement Index for an Australian University Library" (q.v.). Discusses the uses and limitations of the indices described in that article.

Welwood, R. J. "Book Budget Allocations." Canadian Library Journal 34 (June 1977): 213-219.
B113

    Abstract: An objective method for the small academic library to devise allocation formulas for library materials funds. Basic criteria used are enrollment, circulation, and courses taught for each academic area.

Wittig, Glenn R. "Dual Pricing of Periodicals." <u>College and Research Libraries</u> 38 (September 1977): 412-418.

B114

    <u>Abstract</u>: The pervasiveness and nature of dual pricing of periodicals (different subscription price structures for institutions and individuals) is explored, employing a stratified sample of 180 American titles for a span of ten years (1966-75).

Alison, Jennifer. "Serial Prices Double in 12 Years." <u>The Australian Library Journal</u> 25 (June 1976): 179-181.

B115

    <u>Abstract</u>: Compares average serial prices from 1963 to 1975. Gives breakdown by subject for price changes between 1971 and 1975, using <u>Current Australian Serials</u>.

Holland, Maurita Peterson. "Serial Cuts vs. Public Service: a Formula." <u>College and Research Libraries</u> 37 (November 1976): 543-548.

B116

    <u>Abstract</u>: A formula, based on access time, measures the effect of serials budget reduction on public service. It provides librarians with sound justification for major budget cuts.

Axford, William H. "The Validity of Book Price Indexes for Budgetary Projections." <u>Library Resources and Technical Services</u> 19 (Winter 1975): 5-12.

B117

    <u>Abstract</u>: A comparison of the average prices paid for books received through approval plans and the average prices listed annually in the <u>Bowker Annual</u>. Results indicate that the average price paid per title through approval plans is a more reliable guide for budgetary projections than the average price per volume of titles listed in the trade sources.

Burton, Robert E. "Formula Budgeting: An Example." <u>Special Libraries</u> 66 (February 1975): 61-67.

B118

    <u>Abstract</u>: Outlines the development of the Michigan formula for estimating book funds and FTE staffing requirements for academic and research libraries.

Clasquin, F. F. "Serials: Costs and Budget Projections." <u>Drexel Library Quarterly</u> 11 (July 1975): 64-71.

B119

    <u>Abstract</u>: Retrospective price study to analyze serial costs per subject area. Provides a model for allocation of serial funds.

Cohen, Jackson B. "Science Acquisitions and Book Output Statistics." <u>Library Resources and Technical Services</u> 19 (Fall 1975): 370-379.

B120

<u>Abstract</u>: A method for producing statistics for detailed subject analysis of book output and cost statistics for use in planning library resources and determining budget requirements. Currently available statistics are criticized for not being specific enough. Provisional statistics are presented and some examples of the use of these statistics are given.

Gold, Steven D. "Allocating the Book Budget: An Economic Model." <u>College and Research Libraries</u> 36 (September 1975): 397-402.

B121

<u>Abstract</u>: A model is presented in which the division of library resources among competing interests is based upon considerations of economic efficiency.

Kohut, Joseph J. and John F. Walker. "Allocating the Book Budget: Equity and Economic Efficiency." <u>College and Research Libraries</u> 36 (September 1975): 403-410.

B122

<u>Abstract</u>: Gold's cost-benefit model for allocating the book budget is critiqued from the point of view of practicability, economic theory, and equity.

McGrath, William E. "A Pragmatic Book Allocation Formula for Academic and Public Libraries with a Test for Its Effectiveness." <u>Library Resources and Technical Services</u> 19 (Fall 1975): 356-369.

B123

<u>Abstract</u>: A simple and pragmatic empirical book fund allocation procedure using library circulation data and average price of books in subject categories. A test for the effectiveness of allocation is to correlate current buying, or the distribution of books in the shelflist, with the distribution of circulation, using any nonparametric correlation statistic, such as Spearman's rank order statistic.

Merriman, J. B. "Comparative Index to Periodical Prices." <u>Library Association Record</u> 77 (August 1975): 189-190.

B124

<u>Abstract</u>: Annual survey of periodical prices by general subject area.

Randall, Gordon E. "Randall's Rationalized Ratios." <u>Special Libraries</u> 66 (January 1975): 6-11.

B125

Abstract: Statistics on collection size, acquisitions, and interlibrary loans reported by seventeen IBM technical libraries were used to construct acceptable ratios as follows: acquisitions to total collection size; loans to acquisitions; and budget percentages to be allocated among library materials and staff costs. Ratios suggested for use solely in the industrial library environment.

VENDOR PERFORMANCE

Baumann, Susan. "An Extended Application of Davis' 'Model for a Vendor Study.'" <u>Library Acquisitions: Practice and Theory</u> 9 (1985): 317-329.

B126

Abstract: An extension of a dealer performance study (using the model developed by Mary Byrd Davis) by acquisitions department staff of Hunter Library at Western Carolina University to provide a comparison of individual wholesalers' performance over time. As a result of the overall study, the library began to re-examine its profile account and made changes in suppliers for certain types of orders.

Reidelbach, John H. and Gary M. Shirk. "Selecting an Approval Plan Vendor III: Academic Librarians' Evaluations of Eight United States Approval Plan Vendors." <u>Library Acquisitions: Practice and Theory</u> 9 (1985): 177-260.

B127

Abstract: The third of three articles concerning the evaluation and selection of an approval plan vendor for a college or university library. Experiences of more than 100 academic librarians with one or more of eight U. S. approval plan vendors are reported.

Thorton, S. A. and C. J. Bigger. "Periodicals, Prices and Policies." <u>Aslib Proceedings</u> 37 (November/December 1985): 437-452.

B128

Abstract: Reports the results of a survey of 86 special libraries to determine the subscription costs and vendor services provided for 50 scientific and technical journals. Includes check list for determining the cost effectiveness of subscription agent services.

Baumann, Susan. "An Application of Davis' 'Model for a Vendor Study.'" <u>Library Acquisitions: Practice and Theory</u> 8 (1984): 83-90.

B129

    <u>Abstract</u>: A study conducted by the acquisitions department of Hunter Library at Western Carolina University of the eleven book dealers used regularly by the department in order to evaluate vendor performance in relation to library needs. The study resulted in changes in the library's use of certain vendors.

Bracken, James K. and John C. Calhoun. "Profiling Vendor Performance." <u>Library Resources and Technical Services</u> 28 (April/June 1984): 120-128.

B130

    <u>Abstract</u>: Profile of a single vendor's performance, including response time, and sorted by account or subject area and by publisher.

Reidelbach, John H. and Gary M. Shirk. "Selecting an Approval Plan Vendor II: Comparative Vendor Data." <u>Library Acquisitions: Practice and Theory</u> 8 (1984): 157-202.

B131

    <u>Abstract</u>: The second of three articles intended to reduce the time, cost and risk of selecting a domestic approval plan vendor for a college or university library. Comparison of data collected from eight major U. S. approval plan vendors covering: company background, employee background, customer service, profile and title selection, profile maintenance, material forms/slips/returns handling, financial practices, statistical reporting, and miscellaneous data.

Dole, Wanda V. "Austerity and the Arts: Collection Development in the 1980's." <u>Drexel Library Quarterly</u> 19 (Summer 1983): 28-37.

B132

    <u>Abstract</u>: As one type of currently available tool for collection development, describes a cost and coverage study of fine arts titles treated on the approval plans of two vendors.

Green, Paul Robert. "The Performance of Subscription Agents: A Detailed Survey." <u>Serials Librarian</u> 8 (Winter 1983): 7-22.

B133

    <u>Abstract</u>: Uses the number of claims sent for missing journal issues per title and the number of claims per journal issue to judge the performance of subscription agents. Results of 1979 and 1981 studies at the University of Leeds are compared and discussed to provide the basis of an on-going survey.

Perrault, Anna H. "A New Dimension in Approval Plan Service." <u>Library Acquisitions: Practice and Theory</u> 7 (1983): 35-40.
B134

    <u>Abstract</u>: Presents results of a three-month study conducted using the fiche database service offered by a major approval plan vendor and three review tools. The object of the study was to assess the utility of the fiche service to a selector for determining the status of new publications with respect to the library approval program at the time of review. A secondary objective was to assess the usefulness of the fiche service as a tool for monitoring the effectiveness of the vendor's interpretation and implementation of a library's approval plan service.

Reidelbach, John H. and Gary M. Shirk. "Selecting an Approval Plan Vendor: a Step-by-Step Process." <u>Library Acquisitions: Practice and Theory</u> 7
B135 (1983): 115-122.

    <u>Abstract</u>: Describes a practical process for use in evaluating and selecting a domestic approval plan vendor once the decision to use a plan has been made. Details 10 steps including the establishment of preliminary approval plan design, verification of current vendor performance at other comparable academic libraries and notification of the selected vendor.

Green, Paul Robert. "The Performance of Subscription Agents: A Preliminary Survey." <u>Serials Librarian</u> 5 (Summer 1981): 19-24.
B136

    <u>Abstract</u>: Compares performance of subscription agents by determining the number of claims sent for missing journal issues over a set period of time, and by calculating the number of claims per subscription for each agent.

Gregor, Jan and Wendy Carol Fraser. "A University of Windsor Experience with an Approval Plan in Three Subjects and Three Vendors." <u>Canadian</u>
B137 <u>Library Journal</u> 38 (August 1981): 227-231.

    <u>Abstract</u>: Analysis of approval plan vendor performance using the criteria of delivery time, comprehensive subject coverage, and price.

Landesman, Margaret and Christopher Gates. "Performance of American In-Print Vendors: A Comparison at the University of Utah." <u>Library</u>
B138 <u>Acquisitions: Practice and Theory</u> 4 (1980): 287-192.

    <u>Abstract</u>: A comparison of the performance of three domestic book vendors in terms of speed, discount, and service, especially for obscure materials.

Sumler, Claudia, Kristine Barone and Art Goetz. "Getting Books Faster and Cheaper: A Jobber Acquisitions Study." <u>Public Libraries</u> 19 (Winter 1980): 103-105.

B139

<u>Abstract</u>: Report of a six month vendor analysis performed by a regional public library system in Maryland. Two jobbers were compared on the basis of discounts, speed of delivery, and problem-solving ability for selected types of materials. Authors advocate that small public libraries in a region group together and negotiate collectively with jobbers for higher discounts and lower procession costs.

Davis, Mary Byrd. "Model for a Vendor Study in a Manual or Semi-Automated Acquisitions System." <u>Library Acquisitions: Practice and Theory</u> 3 (1979): 53-60.

B140

<u>Abstract</u>: Presents a model for evaluating vendor performance based on the criteria of pricing, speed, fulfillment, and service. The method allows for contrasting individual wholesalers with publishers in general as well as with one another.

Grand, Joan and Susan Perelmuter. "Vendor Performance Evaluation." <u>Journal of Academic Librarianship</u> 4 (1978): 366-367.

B141

<u>Abstract</u>: Analysis of three approval plan vendors by comparing speed, bibliographic accuracy, and discounts.

Lincoln, Robert. "Vendors and Delivery: An Analysis of Selected Publishers, Publisher/Agents, Distributors, and Wholesalers." <u>Canadian Library Journal</u> 35 (February 1978): 51-57.

B142

<u>Abstract</u>: Analysis of delivery time, prices, and supply rates for firm order vendors over a three year period.

Stokley, Sandra L. and Marion T. Reid. "A Study of Performance of Five Book Dealers Used by Louisiana State University Library." <u>Library Resources and Technical Services</u> 22 (Spring 1978): 117-125.

B143

<u>Abstract</u>: A study was conducted to measure the performance of five domestic book dealers during fiscal 1975/76, using detailed analysis of 400 purchase orders from each of the dealers. Results consider discounts and turnaround time as well as other factors.

Hanson, Jo Ann. "An Evaluation of Book Suppliers Used by the University of Denver Library." 1977. ERIC ED156132. Microfiche.

B144

> Abstract: This research project (presented as master's thesis) attempts to provide a basis for systematizing the book ordering process by collecting data on the performance of suppliers used to provide various types of monographic publications for the University of Denver Library and by evaluating this data in terms of speed, reliability, and cost.

Kim, Ung Chon. "Purchasing Books from Publishers and Wholesalers." *Library Resources and Technical Services* 19 (Spring 1975): 133-147.

B145

> Abstract: Book purchase requests for thirty-two titles were sent simultaneously to four different wholesalers and the publishers of the titles. The length of time required for each supplier to provide each of the thirty-two titles was recorded, as well as the charges to the library for each title. The efficiency of each supplier was evaluated in terms of the number of days required to supply books and the percentage of the actual charge against the list price.

CHAPTER 3

SERIALS

GENERAL AND MISCELLANEOUS

C1 Adalian, Paul T., Jr., Ilene F. Rockman and Ernest Rodie. "Student Success in Using Microfiche to Find Periodicals." College and Research Libraries 46 (January 1985): 48-54.

Abstract: Report of a user survey to study student usage of a microfiche serials holdings list to determine the accessibility and retrievability of periodical issues housed in four separate locations in the California Polytechnic State University Library.

C2 Bensman, Stephen J. "Journal Collection Management as a Cumulative Advantage Process." College and Research Libraries 46 (January 1985): 13-29.

Abstract: The paper examines the practical implications of the sociobibliometric laws for the management of journal collections in academic libraries.

C3 Broadus, Robert N. "A Proposed Method for Eliminating Titles from Periodical Subscription Lists." College and Research Libraries 46 (January 1985): 30-35.

Abstract: A method is outlined for determining what periodical titles should be reviewed for cancellation by a university library. A list of candidates for elimination is gathered from titles with low citation counts as found in Journal Citation Reports.

C4 Cullars, John. "Characteristics of the Monographic Literature of British and American Literary Studies." College and Research Libraries 46 (November 1985): 511-522.

Abstract: The aim of this study was to determine how scholars use the monographic literature in British and American literary studies and to compare these findings to those of studies involving the journal literature of the humanities.

Line, Maurice B. "Changes in Rank Lists of Serials Over Time: Interlending versus Citation Data." College and Research Libraries 46 (January 1985): 77-79.

C5

Abstract: Reports on British Library Lending Division surveys of its lending patterns, and compares changes in the rankings among the surveys, as well as comparing the rank list of serials requested with rankings from Journal Citation Reports.

Line, Maurice B. "Use of Citation Data for Periodicals Control in Libraries: A Response to Broadus." College and Research Libraries 46 (January 1985): 36-37. (With response from Broadus, p. 38-39).

C6

Abstract: Response to Broadus' article (College and Research Libraries 46, January 1985) on using low citation-count as a guide to journal cancellations, cautioning careful use of citation counts.

Thomas, Sarah E. "Collection Development at the Center for Research Libraries: Policy and Practice." College and Research Libraries 46 (May 1985): 230-233.

C7

Abstract: This study finds that a significant number of serials currently received by CRL are also held by twenty or more libraries, as indicated by holding symbols on OCLC and RLIN.

Coutts, Brian E. "Newspaper Preferences of Southern ARL Libraries: A Survey." Southeastern Librarian 34 (Fall 1984): 76-78.

C8

Abstract: Describes a survey to determine current newspaper subscriptions maintained by the Southern members of the Association of Research Libraries.

Fjallbrant, Nancy. "Rationalization of Periodical Holdings: A Case Study at Chalmers University Library." Journal of Academic Librarianship 10 (May 1984): 77-86.

C9

Abstract: A study of the use of periodicals in a medium-sized technological university. Aspects examined were use of individual periodicals in relation to language of publication; patterns of use for interlibrary lending and for multiple copy journals; and methods and costs for acquiring infrequently used periodicals (as gift or exchange publications or by purchase), together with availability from other sources.

Goehner, Donna M. "Core Lists of Periodicals Selected by Faculty Reviewers." Technical Services Quarterly 1 (Summer 1984): 17-38.

C10

Abstract: Tabulates choices made by faculty reviewers at 26 medium-sized academic institutions of periodical titles considered to be basic to libraries supporting work at the master's level. Core titles in each subject category are ranked according to frequency of selection.

Goehner, Donna M. "Periodical Coverage in Academic Collections: A Comparison Between Faculty Choices of Core Titles and Holdings of Medium-Sized Libraries." Technical Services Quarterly 1 (Summer 1984): 1-16.

C11

Abstract: Survey analysis comparing subject core periodical lists developed by faculty reviewers against periodical holdings in 26 libraries. Scope of study limited to art, literature, history, psychology, mathematics, and physics periodicals. Results indicate a lack of similarity between periodical titles cited in the faculty core lists and periodical titles available in the libraries surveyed.

Konopasek, Katherine and Nancy Patricia O'Brien. "Undergraduate Periodical Usage: A Model of Measurement." Serials Librarian 9 (Winter 1984): 65-74.

C12

Abstract: Reports a simple and practical method for compiling periodical use in the undergraduate library of the University of Illinois. The study ranked individual periodical titles according to their use, identified the status of the user, identified bound volume use by title and year, and determined loss rate of current issues. Titles satisfying 90% of patron needs also identified.

Preibish, Andre. "Serials Resources in Canadian Research Libraries in 1981." Serials Librarian 8 (Spring 1984): 29-41.

C13

Abstract: Presents data on serial resources in Canadian university, major public, selected college and two national libraries gathered to study budget allocations, new subscriptions and cancellations. The survey indicates some modest growth in serial collections. Discusses the feasibility of a Canadian national serial lending facility.

Turner, Stephen J. and Gregory O'Brien. "A Fuzzy Set Theory Approach to Periodical Binding Decisions." _Journal of the American Society for Information Science_ 35 (July 1984): 228-234.

C14

Abstract: An attempt to apply the fuzzy set theory to the development of a model to aid in bindery decisions. The study tested whether this theory could be applied to a specific collection. Discusses the problems and weaknesses of this kind of application.

Watson, William. "A Periodicals Access Survey in a University Library." _College and Research Libraries_ 45 (November 1984): 496-501.

C15

Abstract: Reports on a survey, conducted on the shelf availability of periodicals in the University of British Columbia Library system, to assess the impact of allowing periodical issues to circulate.

Williams, James. W. "Pre-1950 Serials in OCLC: A Second Look at Database Records and a Comparison with _Union List of Serials_ and _National Union Catalog, Pre-1956 Imprints_." _Serials Librarian_ 8 (Summer 1984): 69-77.

C16

Abstract: Compares the OCLC database with ULS and the NUC Pre-1956 for inclusion of bibliographic data, completeness of information, and number of libraries reporting ownership.

Green, Paul Robert. "The Performance of Subscription Agents: A Detailed Survey." _Serials Librarian_ 8 (Winter 1983): 7-22.

C17

Abstract: Uses the number of claims sent for missing journal issues per title and the number of claims per journal issue to judge the performance of subscription agents. Results of 1979 and 1981 studies at the University of Leeds are compared and discussed to provide the basis of an on-going survey.

Griscom, Richard. "Periodical Use in a University Music Library: A Citation Study of Theses and Dissertations Submitted to the Indiana University School of Music from 1975-1980." _Serials Librarian_ 7 (Spring 1983): 35-52.

C18

Abstract: Reports a citation study of bibliographies in music theses and dissertations conducted at Indiana University that was carried out to measure in-house use of music periodicals. Of the 256 titles cited, only 30% were cited more than once. Periodicals in musicology had a low rate of obsolescence but those in theory and music education had a rate much higher than for the humanities in general.

Holland, Maurita Peterson. "Machine-Readable Files for Serials Management: An Optimizing Program and Use Data." <u>College and Research Libraries</u> 44 (January 1983): 66-69.

C19

<u>Abstract</u>: The files of data created to support use of a formula to assess serial "value" (reported in <u>College and Research Libraries</u> 37, November 1976) are applied to other kinds of objective serials budget analyses.

Lewis, David W. "The Use of Journal Access Service and Its Implications for Journal Selection at the Center for Research Libraries." 1983. ERIC ED234810. Microfiche.

C20

<u>Abstract</u>: Study of journal use at the Center for Research Libraries' Journal Access Service. Analysis of use of a sample of 1010 journal titles from the 1976/77 <u>Ulrich's International Periodicals Directory</u> indicated heavy use of a few titles, 70% English language, and over 50% in science and technology.

Varner, Carroll. "Journal Mutilation in Academic Libraries." <u>Library & Archival Security</u> 5 (Winter 1983): 19-27.

C21

<u>Abstract</u>: An examination of journal mutilation in academic libraries using the number of replacement pages ordered as a measurement of the amount of mutilation occurring.

Williams, Jim and Nancy Romero. "A Comparison of the OCLC Database and New Serial Titles as an Information Resource for Serials." <u>Library Resources and Technical Services</u> 27 (April/June 1983): 188-198.

C22

<u>Abstract</u>: Samples of 200 titles each were drawn from OCLC and NST and each title was searched for a corresponding entry in the other tool. The 217 titles common to both were compared for holdings reports, selected bibliographic data elements, and supplementary notes.

Bryant, Michelle, Elizabeth McKenzie and Roger Fenton. "Magazines in Stir: A Survey of Periodicals at Arohata Youth Institution, Tawa." <u>New Zealand Libraries</u> 43 (December 1982): 205-206.

C23

<u>Abstract</u>: Reports on a survey of the inmates of a women's penal institution about their use of the magazines in the institution's library and their interest in magazines and topics not in the collection. The survey was intended to aid decisions about canceling and adding subscriptions.

Charbonneau, Gary. "Taylor's Constant." <u>Serials Librarian</u> 7 (Fall 1982): 19-22.

C24

Abstract: Estimates frequency with which title changes are made by analyzing a random sample of 1,000 titles from the subscription list of a large university and 250 titles from a public library. Suggests the rate of title change may approach a constant, named Taylor's Constant, of .013 title changes per serial per year.

Gleaves, Edwin S. and Robert T. Carterette. "Microform Serials Acquisition: A Suggested Planning Model." <u>Journal of Academic Librarianship</u> 8 (November 1982): 292-295.

C25

Abstract: A model for estimating expected costs and savings from a microform serials acquisitions program.

Golden, Gary A., Susan U. Golden and Rebecca T. Lenzini. "Patron Approaches to Serials: A User Study." <u>College and Research Libraries</u> 43 (January 1982): 22-30.

C26

Abstract: This study, conducted at a separate serial card catalog in a major research library, measures the success of more than four hundred patrons in the bibliographic retrieval of serials.

Gordon, Martin. "Periodical Use at a Small College Library." <u>Serials Librarian</u> 6 (Summer 1982): 63-73.

C27

Abstract: Analyzes observed uses of general, humanities, social science and science periodicals in Franklin and Marshall College library. Above 90% of total uses adhered to Bradford's Law of Dispersion. General and social science titles had more uses than humanities titles; and indexing, instruction and housing decisions appeared to increase use of any given title. Other analyses were also made.

Peters, Andrew. "Evaluating Periodicals." <u>College and Research Libraries</u> 43 (March 1982): 149-151.

C28

Abstract: The Kraft/Polacsek formula to relate and quantify the factors--such as subject relevance, usage, general availability, indexing, cost, format, publisher reputation, and citation frequency--used in evaluating the worth of a journal to a particular collection, are applied at the Central State University Library.

Stevens, Jana K., Jade G. Kelley and Richard G. Irons. "Cost-Effectiveness of Soviet Serial Exchanges." *Library Resources and Technical Services* 26 (April/June 1982): 151-155.

C29

Abstract: A review of 26 Soviet institutions and 70 Soviet serial publications showed that the availability of Soviet publications through normal trade channels has increased in recent years.

Trubkin, Loene. "Building a Core Collection of Business & Management Periodicals: How Databases Can Help." *ONLINE* 6 (July 1982): 43-49.

C30

Abstract: Analyzes frequency of citation of core journals in business and management by commercial online bibliographic databases. Lists 83 business and management periodicals each of which is cited in five or more online databases.

Green, Paul Robert. "The Performance of Subscription Agents: A Preliminary Survey." *Serials Librarian* 5 (Summer 1981): 19-24.

C31

Abstract: Compares performance of subscription agents by determining the number of claims sent for missing journal issues over a set period of time, and by calculating the number of claims per subscription for each agent.

Mankin, Carole J. and Jacqueline D. Bastille. "An Analysis of the Difference Between Density-of-Use and Raw-Use Ranking of Library Journal Use." *Journal of the American Society for Information Science* 32 (May 1981): 224-228.

C32

Abstract: Proposes using a "density-of-use rank," obtained by dividing raw-use frequency by the linear feet of shelf space used by the title and then ranking the results for serial collection development decisions. Twice as many titles would be needed to include 80% of the total use of the collection as when ranking by raw use is employed. But fewer feet of shelf space would be needed, cost increases are not great, and the number of potential unsatisfied title uses was reduced.

Black, George W. "Statistical Determination of Bound Journal Holdings in a Science Library." *Serials Librarian* 5 (Winter 1980): 31-39.

C33

Abstract: Discusses a method for determining the number of bound journal volumes in a science library using sampling techniques. Allows the calculation of the extent of both current and non-current titles.

White, Herbert S. "Factors in the Decision by Individuals and Libraries to Place or Cancel Subscriptions to Scholarly and Research Journals." *Library Quarterly* 50 (July 1980): 287-309.

C34

Abstract: Describes a survey to gather information on the factors which prompted both individuals and libraries to place new subscriptions or cancel existing subscriptions to established scholarly and research journals.

Flynn, Roger R. "The University of Pittsburgh Study of Journal Usage: A Summary Report." *Serials Librarian* 4 (Fall 1979): 25-33.

C35

Abstract: Presents data on use and costs per use in 6 libraries of the University of Pittsburgh. Results were designed to aid in acquisitions, storage and weeding decisions. The study found that a small percentage of the collections in each library accounted for nearly all the use and that usage was of most recently published volumes.

Fry, Bernard M. and Herbert S. White. "Impact of Economic Pressures on American Libraries and Their Decisions Concerning Scholarly and Research Journal Acquisition and Retention." *Library Acquisitions: Practice and Theory* 3 (1979): 153-237.

C36

Abstract: Survey of economic conditions, budgetary pressures, economic alternatives, behavioral patterns, and actions and perceptions by both librarians and various publisher groups for the years 1974 to 1976. This is an update to the authors' *Publishers and Libraries: A Study of Scholarly and Research Journals*.

Goehlert, Robert. "Journal Use per Monetary Unit: A Reanalysis of Use Data." *Library Acquisitions: Practice and Theory* 3 (1979): 91-98.

C37

Abstract: Analysis of retrospective data to examine the number of uses per monetary unit each journal provides. Monetary unit includes the initial ordering cost and the recurring costs of the subscription, accounting procedures, receiving, binding, and storage.

Key, Jack D., Katherine J. Sholtz and Charles G. Roland. "The Controlled Circulation Journal in Medicine: Rx or Rogue?" *Serials Librarian* 4 (Fall 1979): 15-23.

C38

Abstract: Survey and evaluation of free medical journals to assess readership and value to the collection in the Mayo Clinic Library.

King, Donald W. "Pricing Policies in Academic Libraries." <u>Library Trends</u> 28 (Summer 1979): 47-62.

C39

<u>Abstract</u>: Discussion of the economics of libraries with emphasis on user charges.

Maxin, Jacqueline A. "Periodical Use and Collection Development." <u>College and Research Libraries</u> 40 (May 1979): 248-253.

C40

<u>Abstract</u>: The article gives an example of how use of periodicals in an academic environment has been recorded, how it has been built into a collection development program, and how it has focused on areas for future concern.

Rice, Barbara A. "Science Periodicals Use Study." <u>Serials Librarian</u> 4 (Fall 1979): 35-47.

C41

<u>Abstract</u>: Two semester study of science periodical use at SUNY at Albany to identify little used titles for storage or discard. Even in a large general collection a small core of titles accounted for a large percentage of use. All science journals were included in the study and results were used to cancel subscriptions and discard volumes.

Schloman, Barbara Frick and Ruth E. Ahl. "Retention Periods for Journals in a Small Academic Library." <u>Special Libraries</u> 70 (September 1979): 377-383.

C42

<u>Abstract</u>: Academic departmental library establishes journal retention schedules based on the responses to a questionnaire aimed at its primary users. As a result of the retention schedules, 19% of the collection was removed to secondary storage, titles were identified for cancellation, and a mechanism was implemented for weeding the shelves.

Stenstrom, Patricia and Ruth B. McBride. "Serial Use by Social Science Faculty: A Survey." <u>College and Research Libraries</u> 40 (September 1979): 426-431.

C43

<u>Abstract</u>: The 226 faculty members in the social sciences at the University of Illinois who responded to a survey of their use of serials provided information regarding their serial needs and patterns of use, as well as on the usefulness of specified services.

Warner, Edward S. and Anita L. Anker. "Utilizing Library Constituents Perceived Needs In Allocating Journal Costs." <u>Journal of the American Society for Information Science</u> 30 (November 1979): 325-329.

C44

Abstract: Advocates using constituents perceived needs for titles as a means of ascribing journal collection costs to academic programs, rather than simply using the classification of journals. This also provides more realistic lists of titles in support of a particular academic program.

Weil, S. "Survey on the Use and Cost of Scientific Journals in the Soreq Library." <u>Special Libraries</u> 70 (April 1979): 182-189.

C45

Abstract: Results of a journal use survey conducted at an Israeli research center library to determine whether the budgetary allocation for renewals was justified, and to identify low-use titles which could be cancelled.

Wender, Ruth W. "Counting Journal Title Usage in the Health Sciences." <u>Special Libraries</u> 70 (May/June 1979): 219-226.

C46

Abstract: Report of journal use survey, conducted by the extension division of a university-run health sciences library, that analyzes and compares the interlibrary loan requests of health professionals who receive library services against those health professionals who do not.

Bolgiano, Christina E. and Mary Kathryn King. "Profiling a Periodicals Collection." <u>College and Research Libraries</u> 39 (March 1978): 99-104.

C47

Abstract: Methods for obtaining data about scope, quality, accessibility, and usefulness of existing periodicals collection are presented, including analysis of unmet user needs, comparison with major bibliographies, analysis of accessibility through abstracts and indexes, and determination of the relationship between the collection and the academic programs it supports.

Boyce, Bert R. and Mark Funk. "Bradford's Law and the Selection of High Quality Papers." <u>Library Resources and Technical Services</u> 22 (Fall 1978): 390-401.

C48

<u>Abstract</u>: Describes a comparison of the Bradfordian ranking of journals by their production of papers in a subset of the psychological literature, with the same journals ranked by quality of papers as judged by their frequency of citation. The impact of circulation of a journal and its rejection rate on ranking is also considered.

Broude, Jeffrey. "Journal Deselection in an Academic Environment: A Comparison of Faculty and Librarian Choices." <u>Serials Librarian</u> 3 (Winter 1978): 147-166.

C49

<u>Abstract</u>: Compares titles chosen by faculty for deselection and those chosen by a generalized deselection model representative of a group of librarians and California State University at Dominguez Hills. Little similarity existed between the two sets of choices but the deselection model was felt to be of value in minimizing the degree of subjectivity in cancellation decisions. The model is described and applied.

Clasquin, Frank F. "Financial Management of Serials and Journals Through Subject 'Core' Lists." <u>Serials Librarian</u> 2 (Spring 1978): 287-297.

C50

<u>Abstract</u>: Describes the use of the core list idea for evaluating serials collections and for preparing serials budgets. Comments on the way core lists are constructed and provides examples in the medical field.

Corey, James F. "OCLC and Serials Processing: A State of Transition at the University of Illinois." <u>Serials Librarian</u> 3 (Fall 1978): 57-67.

C51

<u>Abstract</u>: Analysis of the University of Illinois' use of OCLC for pre-order and pre-catalog searching and for full cataloging and card production.

Healey, James S. and Carolyn M. Cox. "Research and the <u>Reader's Guide</u>: An Investigation into the Research Use of Periodicals Indexed in the <u>Reader's Guide to Periodical Literature</u>." <u>Serials Librarian</u> 3 (Winter 1978): 179-190.

C52

<u>Abstract</u>: Analyzes citations from 25 years of theses and dissertations to ascertain research effectiveness of periodicals indexed in the <u>Reader's Guide</u>. Most titles were not used for research and citations tended to occur within 5 years of publication. Questions the long term retention in hard copy or microfilm of many of these titles.

Heroux, Marlene and Carol Fleishauer. "Cancellation Decisions: Evaluating Standing Orders." <u>Library Resources and Technical Services</u> 22 (Fall 1978): 368-379.

C53

<u>Abstract</u>: Describes a methodology for a review of standing orders in the form of a point system that rates titles according to: support of university programs, interlibrary loan availability, language, price, frequency, access by analytics, indexes or abstracts, and circulation. The system is applied to a sample of 109 titles.

Johnson, Carol A. and Richard W. Trueswell. "The Weighted Criteria Statistics Score: An Approach to Journal Selection." <u>College and Research Libraries</u> 39 (July 1978): 287-292.

C54.

<u>Abstract</u>: A practical and systematic technique for journal selection is presented in terms of a weighted criteria statistic score.

Kriz, Harry M. "Subscriptions vs. Books in a Constant Dollar Budget." <u>College and Research Libraries</u> 39 (March 1978): 105-109.

C55

<u>Abstract</u>: Citation analysis was used as an aid in collection development in the field of engineering, to compare the relative usefulness of journals and books to graduate students.

O'Neill, Edward T. "The Effect of Demand Level on the Optimal Size of Journal Collections." <u>Collection Management</u> 2 (Fall 1978): 205-216.

C56

<u>Abstract</u>: Presents a model to determine the optimum size of a collection of journals which will minimize the costs of satisfying the requests of library users. Assumes user requests can be satisfied either by journals in the collection or through inter-library loan.

Seba, Douglas B. and Beth Forrest. "Using SDI's to Get Primary Journals: A New Online Way." ONLINE 2 (January 1978): 10-15.

C57

Abstract: A modified version of Garfield's impact factor formula, incorporating user-determined relevant citation data, is the foundation for an SDI-based journal selection/purchasing model.

Shaw, W. M., Jr. "A Practical Journal Usage Technique." College and Research Libraries 39 (November 1978): 479-484.

C58

Abstract: Describes a practical journal usage technique employed at the Case Western Reserve University Libraries. Further study has resulted in a stable division of the collection into components which are used and not used; a technique for rating the relative liability of the unused titles is also provided.

Cayless, C. F. and C. G. Merritt. "The Keeping Cost of Periodicals." Australian Academic and Research Libraries 8 (December 1977): 178-185.

C59

Abstract: Describes a formula for determining the keeping cost of a serial title (i.e., the cost of getting it into the library and maintaining it, not including subscription cost). The eleven elements of the formula include such things as average annual fixed costs, standard unit times for procedures such as checking and binding, and salary (and overhead) costs per minute of work. The formula focuses on the cost of an individual title, so that differences in keeping cost from title to title may be shown.

Lupton, David Walker. "Serials Subscription Payment Losses: An Analysis." Library Acquisitions: Practice and Theory 1 (January 1977): 3-6.

C60

Abstract: A study of serials payment records from a medium-sized academic library over a nineteen-year period to identify sources of losses and to remind library staff that reviews of payment records are necessary for monitoring and control.

McGregor, James Wilson. "Serials Staffing in Academic Libraries." Serials Librarian 1 (Spring 1977): 259-272.

C61

Abstract: Analysis of experience and educational background of serials workers, the time per title used for serials processing functions, and the number of staff needed for serials processing. Based on investigations of 48 libraries at 9 universities in 1975.

McKenzie, Mary A. "The New England Serials Service: Useful Component of a National System?" <u>Serials Librarian</u> 1 (Spring 1977): 251-258.

C62

    <u>Abstract</u>: Brief description of the New England Serials Service includes some statistical analysis of requests processed and processing time by NESS participants.

Perk, Lawrence J. and Noelle Van Pulis. "Periodical Usage in an Education-Psychology Library." <u>College and Research Libraries</u> 38 (July 1977): 304-308.

C63

    <u>Abstract</u>: A study of periodical usage at the Education-Psychology Library, Ohio State University was conducted using the library's closed reserve system for circulation data. Loan period, binding, multiple copies, closed reserve, and indexing services were considered in relation to actual usage.

Stewart, Blair. "The Cost of Providing Access to Periodical Literature in Academic Libraries." <u>Catholic Library World</u> 49 (September 1977): 70-75.

C64

    <u>Abstract</u>: Discusses the use of the Associated Colleges of the Midwest Periodical Bank by its member libraries and explores the cost effectiveness of such use.

Wenger, Charles B. and Judith Childress. "Journal Evaluation in a Large Research Library." <u>Journal of the American Society for Information Science</u> 28 (September 1977): 293-299.

C65

    <u>Abstract</u>: Reports on 6-month journal evaluation studies at NOAA libraries in Boulder. Data were collected from a use study, circulation and ILL loan statistics, a core list, local availability, questionnaire returns, subscription costs, and patron input. Results showed a 3-month study would have been sufficient and that titles recommended by scientists has a low probability of low use.

Wright, Geraldine Murphy. "Current Trends in Periodical Collections." <u>College and Research Libraries</u> 38 (May 1977): 234-240.

C66

    <u>Abstract</u>: A survey of moderate-sized U. S. academic libraries was conducted to determine current trends in the development and control of periodical collections. Topics covered include selection of new subscriptions, claim procedures, obtaining replacement copies, use of microforms, open versus closed stacks, shelf arrangement, circulation policy, and theft prevention.

Brown, Maryann Kevin and Anita L. McHugh. "Survey of Costs in Technical Processing and Interlibrary Loan." 1976. ERIC ED148358. Microfiche.

C67

Abstract: This report, a part of the Cost and Funding Studies supportive of the development and implementation of western interstate bibliographic network capabilities, summarizes the results of cost data collected in 76 western libraries--public, academic and state. Based upon a stratified sample of 100 libraries, these studies document present costs incurred for cataloging, acquisitions, serials processing and interlibrary loan.

Holland, Maurita Peterson. "Serial Cuts vs. Public Service: A Formula." College and Research Libraries 37 (November 1976): 543-548.

C68

Abstract: A formula, based on access time, measures the effect of serials budget reduction on public service. It provides librarians with sound justification for major budget cuts.

Huff, William H. "Serial Subscription Agencies." Library Trends 24 (April 1976): 683-709.

C69

Abstract: A discussion of the serial subscription agency and its relationship to libraries. Included is a section on costs.

Maxin, Jacqueline A. "Weeding Journals with Informal Use Statistics." The De-acquisitions Librarian 1 (Summer 1976): 9-11.

C70

Abstract: Describes a small college library journal use study which was begun primarily for evaluating subscriptions and developing commercial binding priorities but also proved useful in weeding. Includes forms used to record and tabulate data.

Windsor, Donald A. "De-Acquisitioning Journals Using Productivity/Cost Rankings." The De-acquisitions Librarian 1 (Summer 1976): 1, 8-10.

C71

Abstract: Describes a rank/cost factor study of weeding a journal collection in a small library.

Line, Maurice B. and Alexander Sandison. "Practical Interpretation of Citation and Library Use Studies." College and Research Libraries 36 (September 1975): 393-396.

C72

    Abstract: The paper considers the data required to guide (a) the librarian in acquisition (current and retrospective), discarding, and binding; and (b) the information system designer in selecting journals to be scanned for secondary services, selecting items from journals scanned, and retiring items from active files.

Piternick, Anne B. "Derivation of a Sample of Journal Issues for Tests of Availability and Use." Journal of the American Society for Information Science 26 (September-October 1975): 269-270.

C73

    Abstract: Describes a method of preparing a sample of journal issues for testing purposes. A computer file was created by listing every issue of a set of journals and random samples were then selected by the computer and printed.

Stewart, Blair. "Periodicals and the Liberal Arts College Library." College and Research Libraries 36 (September 1975): 371-378.

C74

    Abstract: Analysis of the periodical holdings of the ten liberal arts college libraries that created the ACM Periodical Bank shows that the "basic list" of periodicals that every such library holds is very short and that these titles are the ones from which the member libraries most frequently requested photocopies.

AUTOMATION

Vogel, J. Thomas and Lynn W. Burns, "Serials Management by Microcomputer: The Potential of DBMS." ONLINE 8 (May 1984): 68-70.

C75

    Abstract: Evaluates the application of PFS file manager software and microcomputer relational DBMS software (dBASE II) to automated serials management in a technical library.

Lundeen, Gerald W. and Charles H. Davis. "Library Automation." Annual Review of Information Science and Technology 17 (1982): 161-186.

C76

    Abstract: Review article covering the years 1980-1981 which looks at library automation. Sections on the technical services are included.

Grosch, Audrey N. "Library Automation." *Annual Review of Information Science and Technology* 11 (1976): 225-266.

C77

    Abstract: Review article on library automation, defined as the application of the computer to routine operations and services in a library. Reference is made to many technical services applications.

Grosch, Audrey. "Serial Arrival Prediction Coding: A Serial Predictive Model for Use by Systems Designers." *Information Processing and Management* 12 (1976): 141-146.

C78

    Abstract: Describes a model that can be used by the designer of serials management systems. Serials arrival, check-in, and claiming functions are included in the model.

COSTS

Emery, Charles D. "Forecasting Models and the Prediction of Periodical Subscription Costs." *Serials Librarian* 9 (Summer 1985): 5-22.

C79

    Abstract: Suggests models that may be used to predict periodical subscription costs and proposes guidelines for designing and implementing a forecasting system. Several selected forecasting models were tested against a time-series of periodical prices, using the mean average deviation as the comparison; the model based on the geometric mean proved most reliable.

Horn, Judith G. and Rebecca T. Lenzini. "Price Indexes for 1985: U. S. Periodicals." *Library Journal* 110 (August 1985): 53-58.

C80

    Abstract: Continuation of annual study of American periodical prices by subject area. Previously compiled by Norman Brown and Jane Phillips.

Joyce, Patrick and Thomas E. Merz. "Price Discrimination in Academic Journals." *Library Quarterly* 55 (July 1985): 273-283.

C81

    Abstract: Analysis of price discrimination, the practice of charging different prices to different customers for the same product, for 89 academic journals. Subject areas covered include chemistry, physics, psychology, economics, sociology, and business.

Lenzini, Rebecca T. "Periodical Prices 1983-1985 Update. "Serials
    Librarian 9 (Summer 1985): 119-130.
C82
    Abstract: Reports Faxon's 3 year comparative price studies for 1983,
    1984, and 1985, with tables and charts similar to previous years.

Ruschin, Siegfried. "Why are Foreign Subscription Rates Higher for
    American Libraries Than They are for Subscribers Elsewhere?" Serials
C83 Librarian 9 (Spring 1985): 7-17.
    Abstract: Compares subscription rates for North American subscribers
    to those charged British, European and other subscribers.

Thornton, S. A. and C. J. Bigger. "Periodicals, Prices and Policies."
    Aslib Proceedings 37 (November/December 1985): 437-452.
C84
    Abstract: Reports the results of a survey of 86 special libraries to
    determine the subscription costs and vendor services provided for 50
    scientific and technical journals. Includes check list for
    determining the cost effectiveness of subscription agent services.

Brown, Norman B. and Jane Phillips. "Price Indexes for 1984: U. S.
    Periodicals and Serial Services." Library Journal 109 (August 1984):
    1422-1425.
-----. "Price Indexes for 1983: U. S. Periodicals and Serial Services."
    Library Journal 108 (September 1, 1983): 1659-1662.
-----. "Price Indexes for 1982: U. S. Periodicals and Serial Services."
    Library Journal 107 (August 1982): 1379-1382.
-----. "Price Indexes for 1981: U. S. Periodicals and Serial Services."
    Library Journal 106 (July 1981): 1387-1393.
-----. "Price Indexes for 1980: U. S. Periodicals and Serial Services."
    Library Journal 105 (July 1980): 1486-1491.
-----. "Price Indexes for 1979: U. S. Periodicals and Serial Services."
    Library Journal 104 (September 1979): 1628-1633.

Brown, Norman B. "Price Indexes for 1978: U. S. Periodicals and Serial
    Services." Library Journal 103 (July 1978): 1356-1361.
-----. "Price Indexes for 1977: U. S. Periodicals and Serial Services."
    Library Journal 102 (July 1977): 1462-1467.
-----. "Price Indexes for 1976: U. S. Periodicals and Serial Services."
    Library Journal 101 (August 1976): 1600-1605.
-----. "Price Indexes for 1975: U. S. Periodicals and Serial Services."
    Library Journal 100 (July 1975): 1291-1295.
C85
    Abstract: Annual study of the cost of American periodicals and serial
    services by subject area. Continued for 1985 by Judith G. Horn and
    Rebecca T. Lenzini.

Hamaker, Charles and Deana Astle. "Recent Pricing Patterns in British Journal Publishing." <u>Library Acquisitions: Practice and Theory</u> 8 (1984): 225-232.

C86

<u>Abstract</u>: A study of the 1984 price lists of seventeen British journal publishers to determine pricing patterns for subscriptions sent to American libraries.

Lenzini, Rebecca T. "Periodical Prices 1982-1984 Update." <u>Serials Librarian</u> 9 (Winter 1984): 13-24.

C87

<u>Abstract</u>: Reports the 3 year comparative price studies for 1982, 1983, and 1984 compiled by the Faxon Company. The tables and analytical charts are generally similar to those presented earlier. The 1984 data are based on 9 rather than 12 months due to a change in Faxon's fiscal year.

Alison, Jennifer. "Recent Australian Serial Prices." <u>Australian Academic and Research Libraries</u> 14 (March 1983): 55-58.

C88

<u>Abstract</u>: Compares average serial prices in 1971, 1975, and 1981, using data from <u>Current Australian Serials</u> and <u>Australian Serials in Print</u>. Gives breakdown by subject for price changes between 1975 and 1981.

Dyl, Edward A. "A Note on Price Discrimination by Academic Journals." <u>Library Quarterly</u> 53 (April 1983): 161-168.

C89

<u>Abstract</u>: Comparative study of prices of academic journals for libraries and for individual subscribers.

Lenzini, Rebecca T. "Periodical Prices 1981-1983 Update." <u>Serials Librarian</u> 8 (Winter 1983): 107-118.

C90

<u>Abstract</u>: Continues the 3 year comparative periodical price studies completed earlier by F. F. Clasquin and Gerald R. Lowell of F. W. Faxon Company. A variety of tables and comparative information is presented.

Lowell, Gerald R. "Periodical Prices 1980-1982 Update." Serials Librarian 7 (Fall 1982): 75-83.

C91

Abstract: An annual update to the 3-year price reviews published by Faxon since 1974; previous updates were published in Library Journal and Serials Librarian. Prices increased an average of 18.5% in 1981 and 9% in 1982.

Clasquin, F. F. "The 1978-80 Faxon Periodical Prices Update." Serials Librarian 5 (Spring 1981): 81-90.

C92

Abstract: Presents average prices and price increases by subject for the 3 year period, 1978 through 1980.

Kronenfeld, Michael R. and James A. Thompson. "The Impact of Inflation on Journal Costs." Library Journal 106 (April 1, 1981): 714-717.

C93

Abstract: Analysis to determine whether or not journal prices rose at a more rapid rate than inflation.

Lowell, Gerald R. "Periodical Prices 1978-1981 Update." Serials Librarian 5 (Spring 1981): 91-99.

C94

Abstract: Continues earlier comparative price studies published by F. F. Clasquin; includes a variety of tables and analytical charts.

Clasquin, F. F. and Jackson B. Cohen. "Biochemistry and Molecular Biology Journal Prices." Serials Librarian 4 (Summer 1980): 381-392.

C95

Abstract: Study of biochemistry and molecular biology journal prices, 1967-1979; demonstrates how these compare in cost to physics and chemistry journals, previously found most costly. A small number of highly cited titles account for nearly 50% of the cost of the entire list of 83 journals studied.

Hentschke, Guilbert C. and Ellen Kehoe. "Serial Acquisition as a Capital Budgeting Problem." Journal of the American Society for Information Science 31 (September 1980): 357-362.

C96

Abstract: Examines costs and benefits of purchasing periodicals on a 1-year versus a 3-year subscription basis--viewed as a capital budgeting problem extending over a six year time span. Critical variables include: cost of capital, subscription reorder costs, annual rate of change of subscription rates and ratio of 1-year to 3-year subscription costs. A model is developed.

Clasquin, F. F. "Periodicals Prices: 77-79 Update." *Library Journal* 104 (October 15, 1979): 2168-2171.

-----. "Periodicals Prices: 76-78 Update." *Library Journal* 103 (October 1, 1978): 1924-1927.

-----. "Periodicals Prices: 75-77 Update." *Library Journal* 102 (October 1, 1977): 2011-2015.

-----. "Periodicals Prices: 1974-76 Update." *Library Journal* 101 (October 1, 1976): 2015-2019.

-----. "Periodicals Prices: 1975 Update." *Library Journal* 100 (October 1, 1975): 1775-1777.

C97

Abstract: Annual comparative study of periodical prices by subject area.

Clasquin, F. F. "Physics and Chemistry Journal Prices in 1977-1978." *Serials Librarian* 3 (Summer 1979): 381-385.

C98

Abstract: Documents the continued double digit inflation for the period 1977 and 1978 for physics and chemistry journals, an extension of the subscription rate increases previously reported for the years 1973 through 1976.

Waltner, Nellie L., Cyrus B. King and William C. Horner. "Periodical Prices: A Comparison of Local and National Averages." *Library Acquisitions: Practice and Theory* 1 (1978): 237-241.

C99

Abstract: A study of average costs for a university library's periodicals in selected Library of Congress classification categories purchased from two major subscription agents.

DeGennaro, Richard. "Escalating Journal Prices: Time to Fight Back." *American Libraries* 8 (February 1977): 69-74.

C100

Abstract: Addresses the ever increasing costs of journals and serials in libraries. Discusses quantitative techniques for managing journal collections as well as ways to cut journal costs.

Wittig, Glenn R. "Dual Pricing of Periodicals." *College and Research Libraries* 38 (September 1977): 412-418.

C101

Abstract: The pervasiveness and nature of dual pricing of periodicals (different subscription price structures for institutions and individuals) is explored, employing a stratified sample of 180 American titles for a span of ten years (1966-75).

Alison, Jennifer. "Serial Prices Double in 12 Years." The Australian
    Library Journal 25 (June 1976): 179-181.
C102

    Abstract: Compare average serial prices from 1963 to 1975. Gives breakdown by subject for price changes between 1971 and 1975, using Current Australian Serials.

Clasquin, F. F. "Serials: Costs and Budget Projections." Drexel Library
    Quarterly 11 (July 1975): 64-71.
C103

    Abstract: Retrospective price study to analyze serial costs per subject area. Provides a model for allocation of serial funds.

Merriman, J. B. "Comparative Index to Periodical Prices." Library
    Association Record 77 (August 1975): 189-190.
C104

    Abstract: Annual survey of periodical prices by general subject area.

CHAPTER 4

CATALOGING

GENERAL AND MISCELLANEOUS

Agnew, Grace, Christina Landram and Jane Richards. "Monograph Arrearages in Research Libraries" *Library Resources and Technical Services* 29 (October/December 1985): 343-359.

D1

Abstract: To determine if backlogs of uncataloged monographs still exist and to learn about methods of controlling and/or reducing any such arrearages, a questionnaire was sent to the 117 members of the Association of Research Libraries; the results are reported.

East, John W. "Citations to Conference Paper and the Implications for Cataloging." *Library Resources and Technical Services* 29 (April/June 1985): 189-194.

D2

Abstract: The citations to fifty conference papers in the field of chemistry, delivered in 1970 and subsequently published, were examined to ascertain the implications of current citation practices for the cataloging of conference proceedings.

Harris, George and Robert Huffman. "Cataloging of Theses: A Survey." *Cataloging & Classification Quarterly* 5 (Summer 1985): 1-15.

D3

Abstract: A survey of the cataloging practices relating to theses and dissertations of the local institution was sent to over 90 academic libraries. Results indicate that where rules exist for cataloging these materials, libraries follow the rules. Where no rules exist, libraries improvise.

Khan, Marta and Jean Tague. "For Canadian Libraries: The Many Forms of Cataloging." *Canadian Library Journal* 42 (February 1985): 17-21.

D4

Abstract: Reports the results of a study of the use of the National Library of Canada's Cataloging-in-Publication (CIP) data by Canadian libraries. The purpose was to determine the extent to which the libraries used CIP data, how they used the data, and to ascertain their perceptions as to the timeliness, accuracy, and comprehensiveness of the data.

McNellis, Claudia Houk. "Describing Reproductions: Multiple Physical Manifestations of the Bibliographical Universe." <u>Cataloging & Classification Quarterly</u> 5 (Spring 1985): 35-48.

D5

<u>Abstract</u>: This project estimated what proportion of a research library's collection existed in multiple physical manifestation throughout the bibliographical universe to attempt to determine whether further research and discussion is justified in the area of the description of reproductions of previously existing works. The MINITAB statistical package was used to analyse the data.

Nichol, W. Thomas. "Theological Subject Headings Reconsidered." <u>Library Resources and Technical Services</u> 29 (April/June 1985): 180-188.

D6

<u>Abstract</u>: In the study reported, all headings in the fifth modified (1982) edition of <u>Catholic Subject Headings</u> were compared with their closest counterparts, if any, in the ninth (1980) edition of <u>LCSH</u> to determine the extent of duplication and the nature of the difference.

Johnson, Karl E. "IEEE Conference Publications in Libraries." <u>Library Resources and Technical Services</u> 28 (October/December 1984): 308-314.

D7

<u>Abstract</u>: Surveys were conducted to determine how libraries handle the conference publications of the Institute of Electrical and Electronics Engineers, the availability of suitable cataloging, and the preference of library patrons regarding access to these publications.

McCrank, Lawrence J. "The Bibliographic Control of Rare Books: Phased Cataloging, Descriptive Standards, and Costs." <u>Cataloging & Classification Quarterly</u> 5 (Fall 1984): 27-51.

D8

<u>Abstract</u>: A survey of the major rare book and manuscript repositories in the U. S. and Canada provides comparative data for the cost of cataloging at levels higher than AACR2 and delineates other characteristics of rare book and special collections operations for personnel, compensation, unit costs, backlogs, regional variance, standards, automation and networking, methods of providing intellectual access, and acquisition activities. The Statistical Package for the Social Sciences (SPSS) was used to analyse the data.

Reeb, Richard. "A Quantitative Method for Evaluating the Quality of
    Cataloging." <u>Cataloging & Classification Quarterly</u> 5 (Winter 1984):
D9 21-26.

   <u>Abstract</u>: As a quality control measure particularly within the
   context of a union database like OCLC, cataloging revision can
   eliminate many errors which might otherwise be input. Based on this
   revision process, a statistical method for evaluating the quality of a
   cataloger's work was developed.

Rutledge, John and Willy Owen. "The Catalog of the Austrian National
    Library as a Bibliographic Resource for U. S. Libraries." <u>Library
D10 Resources and Technical Services</u> 28 (October/December 1984): 325-336.

   <u>Abstract</u>: The study examines use of the microfiche edition of the
   catalog of the Austrian National Library by American libraries. This
   catalog is also compared with other tools, including the <u>National
   Union Catalog</u>.

Truett, Carol. "Is Cataloging a Passe Skill in Today's Technological
    Society?" <u>Library Resources and Technical Services</u> 28 (July/September
D11 1984): 268-275.

   <u>Abstract</u>: A survey was conducted of 200 media specialists in
   Nebraska to determine the extent to which school librarians are
   actually involved in processing both print and nonprint media center
   materials.

Williams, James W. "Pre-1950 Serials in OCLC: A Second Look at Database
    Records and a Comparison with <u>Union List of Serials and National Union
    Catalog, Pre-1956 Imprints</u>." <u>Serials Librarian</u> 8 (Summer 1984): 69-
D12 77.

   <u>Abstract</u>: Compares the OCLC database with ULS and the NUC Pre-1956
   for inclusion of bibliographic data, completeness of information, and
   number of libraries reporting ownership.

Jenkins, Darrell L. "Cataloging Vacancies in Academic Libraries: 'If at
    First You Don't Succeed . . .'" <u>Cataloging & Classification Quarterly</u>
D13 4 (Winter 1983): 41-49.

   <u>Abstract</u>: Reports on a survey about re-opened, extended or "second"
   searches to fill professional cataloging positions in academic
   libraries. The survey covered search procedures, characteristics of
   the applicants, and reasons why the first searches failed.

Seal, Alan. "Experiments With Full and Short Entry Catalogues: A Study of Library Needs." <u>Library Resources and Technical Services</u> 27 (April/June 1983): 144-155.

D14

Abstract: Reports on nine projects at the Center for Catalogue Research on the effectiveness of library catalogs with regard to the level of content of entries.

Albrera, Josefa B. "Bibliographic Structure Possibility Set: A Quantitative Approach for Identifying User's Bibliographic Information Needs." <u>Library Resources and Technical Services</u> 26 (January/March 1982): 21-36.

D15

Abstract: Study to determine the bibliographic control requirements of a small to medium-sized public library from the point of view of the expressed needs of the library patron through telephone and catalog reference. Bibliographic elements in addition to author, title, and subject are identified and all elements are measured as to the extent and use of each for retrieval.

Burgess, Susan Fay. "Job Satisfaction of Reference Librarians and Cataloguers." <u>Australian Academic and Research Libraries</u> 13 (June 1982): 73-81.

D16

Abstract: Reports on a survey in which the Minnesota Satisfaction Questionnaire was used to determine the levels of job satisfaction of full-time reference librarians and full-time catalogers in Australian university libraries.

Charbonneau, Gary. "Taylor's Constant." <u>Serials Librarian</u> 7 (Fall 1982): 19-22.

D17

Abstract: Estimates frequency with which title changes are made by analyzing a random sample of 1,000 titles from the subscription list of a large university and 250 titles from a public library. Suggests the rate of title change may approach a constant, named Taylor's Constant, of .013 title changes per serial per year.

Frohmann, Bernd. "A Bibliometric Analysis of the Literature of Cataloging and Classification." <u>Library Research</u> 4 (1982): 355-373.

D18

Abstract: A quantitative study to identify and investigate a representative sample of the literature of cataloging and classification in order to reveal some of its structural characteristics.

Hassell, Robert H. "Revising the Dewey Music Schedules: Tradition vs. Innovation." Library Resources and Technical Services 26 (April/June 1982): 192-203.

D19

Abstract: Presents a statistical comparison of the music schedules of the Dewey Decimal Classification, and the Library Association's (UK) proposal for a total revision of these schedules. The basis of comparison is a random sample of 400 chamber-music scores from the British Catalogue of Music. Each classification is analyzed for its strengths and weaknesses in terms of its ability to meet the needs of performers.

Marliw, Michael. "Distribution of Subject Headings in an On-line Academic Library Catalog." American Society for Information Science Proceedings 19 (1982): 186-188.

D20

Abstract: Examines the distribution of subject headings in the online catalog of Ohio State University libraries. Patterns established in this catalog are compared to the OCLC data base and similarities and differences between the two are noted.

McDonough, Joyce G., Carol Alf O'Connor and Thomas A. O'Connor. "Moving the Backlog: An Optimum Cycle for Searching OCLC." Library Acquisitions: Practice and Theory 6 (1982): 265-270.

D21

Abstract: Report of a three year study conducted to determine the optimum number of times an item should be searched on OCLC and an appropriate time frame for the performance of those searches.

Mendenhall, Kathryn. "A Survey of the Cataloging in Publication Program. Final Report." 1982 ERIC ED221215. Microfiche.

D22

Abstract: Report of a survey of 2,366 randomly selected U. S. libraries, describing the use and impact of the CIP program. Results reveal heavy use of CIP in technical services and little use in public services. Extensive use of tables present the results of the survey.

Overmier, Judith A. and Elizabeth Ihrig. "Eighteenth-Century Short-Title Catalogue: A Medical Model of the Costs of Participation by Specialized Collections." College and Research Libraries 43 (November 1982): 445-449.

D23

Abstract: This paper uses the medical school library rare-book collection as a model to familiarize specialized collections with the ESTC/NA project and the value of their contributions to it.

Tayyeb, Rashid. "Implementing AACR2--A National Survey." <u>Canadian Library Journal</u> 39 (December 1982): 373-376.

D24

<u>Abstract</u>: Survey of the ways in which Canadian libraries implemented the <u>Anglo-American Cataloguing Rules</u> (2nd edition).

Dale, Doris Cruger. "Cataloging and Classification Practices in Community College Libraries." <u>College and Research Libraries</u> 42 (July 1981): 333-340.

D25

<u>Abstract</u>: Results of a questionnaire survey sent to a sample of community college libraries to determine cataloging, classification and organizational practices.

Dole, Wanda V. "Processing Architectural Drawings Collections." <u>Southeastern Librarian</u> 31 (Fall 1981): 107-109.

D26

<u>Abstract</u>: Survey of 117 architectural libraries concerning the processing, indexing, and storage of collections of architectural drawing.

Hendrickson, Leslie and Marie Celestre. "An Evaluation of an Oregon School District's Centralized Ordering and Processing System." <u>Library Resources and Technical Services</u> 25 (April/June 1981): 162-176.

D27

<u>Abstract</u>: This evaluation of a medium-sized school district's centralized ordering and processing system was undertaken to investigate complaints about time lags in the operation of the system. Data were collected through interviews, questionnaires, and a random sample search of ordering and processing records.

Mikita, Elizabeth G. "Monographs in Microform: Issues in Cataloging and Bibliographic Control." <u>Library Resources and Technical Services</u> 25 (October/December 1981): 352-361.

D28

<u>Abstract</u>: The magnitude of the problem of local bibliographic control of microforms is identified, the history of attitudes and practices regarding the cataloging of microforms is reviewed, and it is suggested that integrated bibliographic access be implemented at local and national levels.

Nemchek, Lee R. "Problems of Cataloging and Classification in Theater Librarianship" <u>Library Resources and Technical Services</u> 25
D29 (October/December 1981): 374-385.

Abstract: Survey identifies unsuitability of existing classification systems for use with theater collections, and difficulties, due to low budgets, of cataloging "fugitive" theatrical memorabilia.

O'Neill, Edward T. and Rao Aluri. "Library of Congress Subject Heading Patterns in OCLC Monographic Records." <u>Library Resources and</u>
D30 <u>Technical Services</u> 25 (January/March 1981): 63-80.

Abstract: This investigation examined the characteristics of subject headings found in OCLC cataloging records. The study analyzed a sample of 33,455 monographic records, which contained a total of 50,213 subject headings, 94% of which were LC subject headings.

Taylor, Arlene G. "The Impact of AACR2: A Review of Research." <u>Library Research</u> 3 (Summer 1981): 107-122.
D31

Abstract: A review article summarizing AACR2 impact studies, methodology used, results of studies, etc.

Pang, Isabel S. "How AACR2 Will Affect a Medium-Sized Library." <u>Journal of Academic Librarianship</u> 6 (September 1980): 208-209.
D32

Abstract: A study to measure the impact of AACR2 on the catalog of a medium sized college library using data from changes announced by the Library of Congress.

Roughton, Michael. "OCLC Serials Records: Errors, Omissions, and Dependability." <u>Journal of Academic Librarianship</u> 5 (January 1980):
D33 316-321.

Abstract: A examination of serial records in OCLC for accuracy and completeness.

Ryans, Cynthia C. "Cataloging Administrators' Views on Cataloging Education" <u>Library Resources and Technical Services</u> 24 (Fall 1980): 343-351.

D34

<u>Abstract</u>: Reports the results of a survey of cataloging practitioners on their opinions on the following issues: 1) structure of the cataloging curriculum in today's graduate library school; 2) relationship of the use of computers in cataloging to the cataloging curriculum; and 3) adequacy of preparation of current graduates for positions as catalog librarians.

Schadlich, Thomas. "Changing from Sears to LC Subject Headings." <u>Library Resources and Technical Services</u> 24 (Fall 1980): 361-363.

D35

<u>Abstract</u>: Discusses the factors that might induce a library to consider changing from Sears to LC subject headings, and provides a quantitative evaluation of the compatibility of Sears and LC headings.

Tenopir, Carol and Margaret Johnson. "OCLC Card Receipts." <u>Journal of Library Automation</u> 13 (June 1980): 136-138.

D36

<u>Abstract</u>: Studies the average number of days for the receipt of OCLC cards through the U. S. Postal Service in a period of seven and one-half months. Findings showed overall 26 days were required for a combination of first class rate and library rate.

Anderson, Sandy E. and Carol A. Melby. "Comparative Analysis of the Quality of OCLC Serials Cataloging Records, as a Function of Contributing CONSER Participant and Field, as Utilized by Serials Catalogers at the University of Illinois." <u>Serials Librarian</u> 3 (Summer 1979): 363-371.

D37

<u>Abstract</u>: Demonstrates statistically the extent to which serials cataloging copy from OCLC can be accepted without modification at the University of Illinois. Two groups of data were analyzed to determine the nature and frequency of required modifications. A test was also made to determine the extent that LC copy was accepted without modification as compared to copy input by CONSER participants.

Martin, Barbara and Earl P. Smith. "Materials Processing: Centralized Versus the Individual School, a Continuing Controversy." 1979. ERIC ED200242. Microfiche.

D38

Abstract: A two-part survey was conducted in a large school district to determine the kind and extent of centralized versus individual school materials processing with attention focused on long- and short-range implications.

Rogers, JoAnn V. "Mediatmosphere: Nonprint Cataloging: A Call for Standardization." American Libraries 10 (January 1979): 46-48.

D39

Abstract: Results of a survey of school librarians and media specialists on the descriptive cataloging of multimedia materials in school collections.

Comaromi, John P. "Use of the Dewey Decimal Classification in the United States and Canada." Library Resources and Technical Services 22 (Fall 1978): 402-408.

D40

Abstract: A summary of a survey of the use of the DDC in the U. S. and Canadian libraries is presented, including percentage of libraries using DDC, and views on the revision of DDC and its index.

Corey, James F. "OCLC and Serials Processing: A State of Transition at the University of Illinois." Serials Librarian 3 (Fall 1978): 57-67.

D41

Abstract: Analysis of the University of Illinois' use of OCLC for pre-order and pre-catalog searching and for full cataloging and card production.

Kayner, Nedra L. "Unit Time/Cost Study of the Cataloging Unit, Technical Services Division, Tucson Public Library." 1978. ERIC ED194091. Microfiche.

D42

Abstract: The second of three Technical Services studies designed to determine unit time and cost estimates for the Cataloging Unit's activities.

Stecher, G. "Blackwell/North America Title Index at VLU." *Australian Academic and Research Libraries* 9 (March 1978): 48-51.

D43

Abstract: Describes an experiment at La Trobe University in which a sample of titles was searched in the BNA Index and the National Union Catalog, and the annual savings from using the BNA Index projected, based on hit rates, searching time, and the lower cost of cataloging with MARC records. In addition, the distribution of records by country and date of publication was analyzed.

Wellisch, Hans H. "Multiscript and Multilinqual Bibliographic Control: Alternatives to Romanization." *Library Resources and Technical Services* 22 (Spring 1978): 179-189.

D44

Abstract: The implications of separation of catalogs by script and the separation of entries in non-Roman scripts by language are explored. Data on present book production are considered.

Patterson, Kelly, Carol White and Martha Whittaker. "Thesis Handling in University Libraries." *Library Resources and Technical Services* 21 (Summer 1977): 274-285.

D45

Abstract: Libraries of ninety universities granting doctorates were surveyed regarding binding, cataloging, classification, storage, and checking of format practices for theses and dissertations.

Sleep, Esther L. "Whither the ISSN? A Practical Experience." *Canadian Library Journal* 34 (August 1977): 265-270.

D46

Abstract: Examination of the International Standard Serial Number (ISSN) as a reliable, unique identifier for serial titles.

Brown, Maryann Kevin and Anita L. McHugh. "Survey of Costs in Technical Processing and Interlibrary Loan." 1976. ERIC ED148358. Microfiche.

D47

Abstract: This report, a part of the Cost and Funding Studies supportive of the development and implementation of western interstate bibliographic network capabilities, summarizes the results of cost data collected in 76 western libraries--public, academic and state. Based upon a stratified sample of 100 libraries, these studies document present costs incurred for cataloging, acquisitions, serials processing and interlibrary loan.

Bourne, Charles P. "Analysis of Errors in the University of California Union Catalog Supplement." June 1976 ERIC ED127922. Microfiche.

D48

Abstract: Examination of the error rate in a computer produced book catalog. Presents a methodology for studying error rates in large bibliographic files.

Brock, Joan, Doris Paterson and Patricia Alexander. "Survey of Current Staffing Practice in Public Libraries." New Zealand Libraries 38 (April 1975): 74-85.

D49

Abstract: Reports on a survey of New Zealand public libraries about staffing practice, and measures that practice against New Zealand Library Association standards for number and qualifications of staff. Covers all staff, but has breakdowns for catalogers and for commercial and technical librarians.

AUTHORITY CONTROL

Papakhian, Arsen R. "The Frequency of Personal Name Headings in the Indiana University Music Library Card Catalogs." Library Resources and Technical Services 29 (July/September 1985): 273-285.

D50

Abstract: Previous studies of general library catalogs have found that about two-thirds of the personal name headings occur only once. The card catalogs of the Indiana University Music Library were sampled to see if this observation applied in the case of a special materials catalog.

Cook, C. Donald. "Headings for Corporate Names: International Standardization under AACR2." Library Resources and Technical Services 28 (July/September 1984): 239-252.

D51

Abstract: To test the extent and kind of international standardization resulting from the use of the second edition of AACR, a study was made of catalogue headings for corporate names entered in direct order.

Dickson, Jean. "An Analysis of User Errors in Searching an Online
　　　Catalog." <u>Cataloging & Classification Quarterly</u> 4 (Spring 1984): 19-
D52　38.

　　　<u>Abstract</u>:　The study extracts a sample of zero-hit author and title
　　　searches from the transaction log of Northwestern University Library's
　　　online catalog.　It analyzes why the searches failed, in an effort to
　　　understand the user's conceptual model of the online catalog.

Shore, Melinda L.　"Variation Between Personal Name Headings and Title Page
　　　Usage."　<u>Cataloging & Classification Quarterly</u> 4 (Summer 1984): 1-11.
D53
　　　<u>Abstract</u>: Examines the extent and kind of variation between personal
　　　name headings in the catalog and the way author's names are used on
　　　title pages in an effort to add to the knowledge required to decide
　　　whether authority control in an online environment is needed or
　　　justified.　The data were tabulated using the MINITAB Statistical
　　　package.

Taylor, Arlene G.　"Authority Files in Online Catalogs:　An Investigation
　　　of Their Value."　<u>Cataloging & Classification Quarterly</u> 4 (Spring
D54　1984): 1-17.

　　　<u>Abstract</u>: Authority control is discussed from two viewpoints.　Data
　　　from two research projects that support the need for choosing one form
　　　of name are summarized.　The author's study of user requests that
　　　resulted in no "hits" in an online catalog is described.　Data are
　　　given to show that for only 6.4% of those requests would our current
　　　methods of cross referencing in authority records have been helpful,
　　　and that two system programs would have given much assistance.

Thomas, Catherine M.　"Authority Control in Manual Versus Online Catalogs:
　　　An Examination of 'See' References."　<u>Information Technology and</u>
D55　<u>Libraries</u> 3 (December 1984):　393-398.

　　　<u>Abstract</u>: Compares two authority control systems in terms of cross
　　　references and evaluates the differences as related to the use of
　　　online key-word search.　Results show that 47% of the cross references
　　　made for a manual catalog would not be necessary in an online
　　　environment.

Hostage, John. "AACR 2, OCLC, and the Card Catalog in the Medium-Sized Library." <u>Library Resources and Technical Services</u> 26 (January/March 1982): 12-30.

D56

Abstract: The impact of AACR 2 on the card catalog in a medium-sized library was analyzed in a study using a random sample from a year's cataloging. Rates of conflict, amount of corrections, and creation of split files were considered under different scenarios.

Finks, Lee W. and Minoo Pejman. "The Impact of AACR2 on Public Library Catalogs." <u>Public Libraries</u> 20 (Winter 1981): 107-109.

D57

Abstract: Random sampling of revised headings supports authors' premise that most catalog entry conflicts can be resolved with minimal shifting of cards.

McCallum, Sally H. "Statistics on Headings in the MARC File." <u>Journal of Library Automation</u> 14 (September 1981): 194-201.

D58

Abstract: Library of Congress MARC II files from 1969 through October 1979 were analyzed to gain information on characteristics of headings, expected sizes and growth rates of various subsets of authority files. Study was done to support the Network Development Office of LC in the design requirements of a national authority file.

Byrum, John D. and Richard J. Ricard, Jr. "AACR 1 as Applied by Research Libraries to Determine Entry and Headings." <u>Library Resources and Technical Services</u> 24 (Winter 1980): 25-43.

D59

Abstract: In 1975, the research library community was surveyed concerning its adoption and application of AACR 1 for determining entry and heading. Various techniques for adopting it are discussed, including superimposition.

Kline, Peggy S. and Marion R. Taylor. "Adapting an Existing Card Catalog to AACR 2: A Feasibility Study." <u>Library Resources and Technical Services</u> 24 (Summer 1980): 209-213.

D60

Abstract: The feasibility of adapting a given card catalog to AACR 2 was tested by examining all personal and corporate name access points in a sample of recently catalogued titles. Kinds of changes and extent of disruption to the filing sequence were considered in setting criteria for four types of action.

Potter, William Gray. "When Names Collide: Conflict in the Catalog and
    AACR2." <u>Library Resources and Technical Services</u> 24 (Winter 1980):
D61 3-16.

    <u>Abstract</u>: Application of Lotka's Law (percentage of authors producing one journal article in a field) to personal authors in the card catalog. Two card catalogs were sampled, as well as personal author entries for new titles. The implications of the findings for the adoption of AACR 2 are discussed.

Walker, Virginia. "Combining Two Subject Heading Lists in One Catalog:
    Problems for Patrons." <u>Public Library Quarterly</u> 1 (Summer 1979):
D62 139-146.

    <u>Abstract</u>: Describes a study of the difference between Sears and LC subject headings based on a random sample of 663 book titles held by a public library using both systems in its card catalog.

<u>AUTOMATION</u>

Coyle, Karen and Linda Gallaher-Brown. "Record Matching: An Expert
    Algorithm." <u>American Society for Information Science Proceedings</u> 22
D63 (1985): 77-80.

    <u>Abstract</u>: Gives a general description of a statistical algorithm for computer matching of catalog records produced in different libraries for the same work. Since the algorithm involves a weighted evaluation of data elements in the catalog records, it can compensate for minor differences in field content, missing data elements, and variations in cataloging practice. The algorithm is used for adding records to the online union catalog of the University of California.

Dobrovitz, P. "Computerization and the Future of ABN in the UNSW Library."
    <u>Australian Academic and Research Libraries</u> 16 (September 1985): 139-
D64 145.

    <u>Abstract</u>: Gives figures showing that automation substantially increased the productivity of catalogers at the University of New South Wales Library between 1963 and 1983. Argues in favor of participation in the Australian Bibliographic Network.

Bowerman, Roseann and Susan A. Cady. "Government Publications in an Online Catalog: A Feasibility Study." *Information Technology and Libraries* 3 (December 1984): 331-341.
D65

Abstract: Explores the feasibility of including bibliographic records for U. S. documents in an online public access catalog. Reports the survey results of libraries and related organizations that use GPO MARC records. Compares four methods of obtaining GPO MARC records on the basis of initial costs, recurring costs, and quality.

Knutson, Gunnar. "Use Study of Online Cataloging in a Special Library." *Special Libraries* 75 (January 1984): 36-43.
D66

Abstract: Statistical analysis of the original cataloging records of a municipal reference library to determine their use by OCLC member libraries.

Hillman, Diane and Christopher Sugnet. "Comparison of OCLC and RLIN: A Question of Quality." *Cataloging & Classification Quarterly* 4 (Fall 1983): 65-72.
D67

Abstract: A followup (to a study of the cost of quality cataloging in a library using OCLC done in 1979 by Christian M. Boissonnas) to determine whether the differences in design and membership of bibliographic utilities has any measurable effect on the quality of the records.

Leung, Shirley W. "MARC CIP Records and MARC LC Records: An Evaluative Study of Their Discrepancies." *Cataloging & Classification Quarterly* 4 (Winter 1983): 27-39.
D68

Abstract: Reports on a study to determine the frequency and types of discrepancy between MARC CIP records and subsequent MARC LC records. The Statistical Analysis System (SAS) Program was used to analyse the data.

Lundeen, Gerald W. and Charles H. Davis. "Library Automation." *Annual Review of Information Science and Technology* 17 (1982): 161-186.
D69

Abstract: Review article covering the years 1980-1981 which looks at library automation. Sections on the technical services are included.

New York State Library, and others. "Research Library Resources Access Project: Final Report. A Retrospective Conversion Project." 1982.
D70 ERIC ED217843. Microfiche.

Abstract: Description of a 3-year retrospective catalog conversion project for monographic records from six major New York State research libraries into machine-readable format using OCLC.

Wanninger, Patricia Dwyer. "Is the OCLC Database Too Large? A Study of the Effect of Duplicate Records in the OCLC System." Library
D71 Resources and Technical Services 26 (October/December 1982): 353-361.

Abstract: Reports on a study exploring the extent to which duplicates in the OCLC database are affecting the usefulness of the system.

Williams, Martha E. and others. "MARC Database Statistics: An Aid to BSDP Participants Covering Volumes 1 through 8 of the LC MARC Database
D72 BOOKS ALL. Final Report." 1982. ERIC ED234782. Microfiche.

Abstract: Analysis of MARC records from 1973 to 1981 based on record length, field of occurance, data element length per field tag, and classification by Dewey Decimal or Library of Congress schedule. Extensive tables. Data may prove useful to planners of machine-readable catalog files and MARC file users.

Crowe, William J. "Cataloging Contributed to OCLC: A Look One Year Later." Library Resources and Technical Services 25 (January/March
D73 1981): 56-62.

Abstract: Report on a study to examine the disposition, one year after input, of a sample of original cataloging contributed to the OCLC data base by the Indiana University, Bloomington, Libraries, and the degree to which records were superseded or duplicated by LC cataloging.

Druschel, Joselyn. "Cost Analysis of an Automated and Manual Cataloging and Book Processing System." Journal of Library Automation 14 (March
D74 1981): 24-49.

Abstract: Presents a comparative cost analysis of an automated network system (WLN) and a manual system of cataloging and book processing by using a per-unit cost approach. Presents the process and results of the analysis in a series of charts showing tasks, items processed, unit and total monthly costs of both systems. Study shows the manual system is 20% more costly than the automated system.

Hudson, Judith. "Revisions to Contributed Cataloging in a Cooperative
     Cataloging Database. _Journal of Library Automation_ 14 (June 1981):
D75 116-120.

   Abstract: Analyzes 1,017 member contributed monographic catalog
   records in the OCLC database to determine if quality of contributed
   cataloging had improved as a result of recent quality control
   developments. Findings showed slight improvement in error rate when
   compared to that of an earlier study.

Johnson, Judith J. and Clair S. Josel. "Quality Control and the OCLC Data
     Base: A Report on Error Reporting." _Library Resources and Technical_
D76 _Services_ 25 (January/March 1981): 40-47.

   Abstract: The study is designed to provide librarians with a
   practical guide for reaching an informed policy decision on the
   question of submitting error reports to OCLC for database quality
   control. It addresses the questions: 1) what types of errors,
   changes, or additions should be reported? 2) once reported, will
   errors be corrected promptly? and 3) what is the cost of error
   reporting?

Moore, Barbara. "Patterns in the Use of OCLC by Academic Library
     Cataloging Departments" _Library Resources and Technical Services_ 25
D77 (January/March 1981): 30-39.

   Abstract: A survey of the cataloging departments of 166 OCLC member
   academic libraries showed the degree of exclusive reliance on OCLC for
   card production, and the rate of acceptance of non-LC OCLC records
   with or without substantial checking.

Rastogi, Kunj B. and Ichiko T. Morita. "OCLC Search Key Usage Patterns in
     a Large Research Library." _Journal of Library Automation_ 14 (June
D78 1981): 90-99.

   Abstract: Studies the actual search keys entered by users of the OCLC
   online system to determine user preference and effectiveness of the
   preferred search keys.

Baldwin, Paul E. and Leigh Swain. "RECON Alternatives for Eight British Columbia Public Libraries: An Ancillary Report for the British Columbia Library Network . . . " 1980. ERIC ED200207. Microfiche.

D79

Abstract: Feasibility study to estimate alternative costs in 1980 Canadian dollars of using four bibliographic utilities to accomplish retrospective conversion of the manual card files of eight British Columbia public libraries and to make a recommendation about which to use.

Braden, Sally, John D. Hall and Helen H. Britton. "Utilization of Personnel and Bibliographic Resources for Cataloging by OCLC Participating Libraries." Library Resources and Technical Services 24 (Spring 1980): 135-154.

D80

Abstract: On the basis of a survey of 147 OCLC member academic libraries, statistics are presented on 1) cataloging production on a first time use basis; 2) size of professional and support staff; 3) utilization of staff and bibliographic resources for cataloging; 4) adherence to the AACR and LC practice, and 5) extent of verification of OCLC member records. Trends toward less verification of member records and increased use of support staff are identified.

Metz, Paul and John Espley. "The Availability of Cataloging Copy in the OCLC Data Base." College and Research Libraries 41 (September 1980): 430-436.

D81

Abstract: A sixteen-week longitudinal study was conducted to determine the effectiveness of OCLC as a source of cataloging data and to optimize the timing of searches for cataloging copy for various categories of materials.

Roughton, Michael. "OCLC Serials Records: Errors, Omissions, and Dependability." Journal of Academic Librarianship 5 (January 1980): 316-321.

D82

Abstract: An examination of serial records in OCLC for accuracy and completeness.

Kershner, Lois M. "Impact of the BALLOTS Shared Cataloging System on the Amount of Change in the Library Technical Processing Department." 1979. ERIC ED176786. Microfiche.

D83

Abstract: The amount of change resulting from the implementation of the BALLOTS system in 44 libraries of all types is analyzed, in terms of 1) physical room arrangement, 2) work procedure, and 3) organizational structure. Also considered is the factor of the amount of time the system has been in use.

Matthews, Fred W. "Library Catalogue Automation: Cost-Benefit Factors." 1979. ERIC ED180485. Microfiche.

D84

Abstract: Description of an automated card catalog system, developed for the Dartmouth Regional Library in Nova Scotia, which uses records of selected fixed-length fields. The costs of operating a system based on MARC-type records and one using selected fixed-length fields are compared.

Shaw, Debora and Edward A. Stockey. "Contributions of Small Libraries to State-Wide Resource Sharing: A Study of Collection Overlap Through the INCOLSA Processing Center." Public Library Quarterly 1 (Fall 1979): 281-290.

D85

Abstract: An analysis of the INCOLSA Processing Center file to determine public library collection overlap as well as to evaluate the file's utility as a resource sharing tool.

Shaw, Debora and Charles H. Davis. "Cooperation Cataloging and Automated Bibliographic Networks; Consideration for Public Libraries." Public Library Quarterly 1 (Winter 1979): 387-397.

D86

Abstract: Examination of the collection overlap between eight public library collections in the United States and Canada utilizing the OCLC database.

Tracy, Joan I. and Barbara Remmerde. "Availability of Machine-Readable Cataloging: Hit Rates for BALLOTS, BNA, OCLC and WLN for the Eastern Washington University Library." Library Research 1 (Fall 1979): 277-281.

D87

Abstract: A sample of titles from the collection of the Eastern Washington University Library was searched in four machine-readable bibliographic databases with results of searches summarized.

Williams, Martha E., Stephen W. Barth and Scott E. Preece. "Summary Statistics for Five Years of the MARC Data Base." *Journal of Library Automation* 12 (December 1979): 314-337.

D88

Abstract: MARC tapes covering 5 years were analyzed for statistics pertaining to record lengths, field tag occurrences, data element lengths per field tag, and distribution of records by Dewey Decimal Division and the Library of Congress class codes.

Pierce, Anton R. and Joe K. Taylor. "A Model for Cost Comparison of Automated Cataloging Systems." *Journal of Library Automation* 11 (March 1978): 6-23.

D89

Abstract: Develops a model to calculate costs of automated cataloging systems using OCLC and BALLOTS as examples. These two were compared to the costs of an existing manual system.

Ryans, Cynthia C. "A Study of Errors Found in Non-MARC Cataloging in a Machine-Assisted System." *Journal of Library Automation* 11 (June 1978): 125-132.

D90

Abstract: Reports on a study which analyzed the cataloging records input into the OCLC database by member libraries in order to determine where most errors occurred as well as the type of errors.

Landram, Christina. "Cataloging: OCLC Terminal Plus Printer." *Library Resources and Technical Services* 21 (Spring 1977): 147-155.

D91

Abstract: Procedures of a system using a printer in conjunction with an OCLC terminal are described, and advantages are listed regarding the use of the printer versus on-line cataloging. Statistics are presented relative to searching procedures and percentages of titles found in the data base. A comparison of this method with the former one using LC cards is included.

Meyer, R. W. and Rebecca Panetta. "Two Shared Cataloging Data Bases: A Comparison." *College and Research Libraries* 38 (January 1977): 19-24.

D92

Abstract: The OCLC and Blackwell North America data bases are compared for availability of cataloging for English language books. Costs and peripheral services are also compared.

Morita, Ichiko T. and D. Kaye Gapen. "A Cost Analysis of the Ohio College Library Center On-line Shared Cataloging System in the Ohio State University Libraries." *Library Resources and Technical Services* 21 (Summer 1977): 286-302.

D93

Abstract: A study of the costs of cataloging and associated processing tasks before and after the adoption of OCLC at the Ohio State University Libraries compares production on-line with manual procedures, and compares unit cost increases with the general rate of inflation.

Reid, Marion T. "Effectiveness of the OCLC Data Base for Acquisitions Verification." *Journal of Academic Librarianship* 2 (January 1977): 303, 326.

D94

Abstract: A study to evaluate the effectiveness of the OCLC database as an acquisitions verification tool in comparison to conventional library search tools.

Ross, Ryburn M. "Cost Analysis of Automation in Technical Services." In *The Economics of Library Automation*, 1976 Clinic on Library Applications of Data Processing, pp. 10-27. Urbana: University of Illinois Graduate School of Library and Information Science, 1977.

D95

Abstract: Develops costs for automation activities, with specific information on cataloging costs before and after automation. Presents some information on productivity measurement and proposes techniques to measure technical services staff performance.

Shoemaker, Thomas P. "Public Library Automation Network: A Cost/Benefit Analysis of the PLAN Project." 1977. ERIC ED156106. Microfiche.

D96

Abstract: Information is presented on the experiences, benefits, and impact costs of the PLAN Project for public libraries in California. System benefits and problems as related to areas in library technical processing affected by BALLOTS are identified and discussed.

Grosch, Audrey N. "Library Automation." *Annual Review of Information Science and Technology* 11 (1976): 225-266.

D97

Abstract: Review article on library automation, defined as the application of the computer to routine operations and services in a library. Reference is made to many technical services applications.

Stecher, G. "OCLC Reviewed." <u>Australian Academic and Research Libraries.</u> 7 (September 1976): 200-201.

D98

<u>Abstract</u>: Letter that serves as a footnote to G. Stecher's "Shared Cataloguing: An Exercise in Costing OCLC" (below). Gives highlights of two studies of OCLC. Not itself a statistical article.

Stecher, G. "Shared Cataloguing: An Exercise in Costing OCLC." <u>Australian Academic and Research Libraries</u> 7 (March 1976): 1-11.

D99

<u>Abstract</u>: Criticizes available studies of the impact of OCLC. Describes a method for projecting the financial impact of using OCLC in pre-catalog searching, cataloging proper, and card production at La Trobe University. Bases rough estimates of cost and savings per title on regular work and budget statistics, sampling, and empirical estimates.

Williams, Martha E. "Data Element Statistics for the MARC II Data Base." <u>Journal of Library Automation</u> 9 (June 1976): 89-100.

D100

<u>Abstract</u>: Analyzes the statistics of the MARC II database for 1974-75 showing data element occurrences, lengths, distribution records by Dewey Decimal Division and by Library of Congress class codes.

<u>RETROSPECTIVE CONVERSION</u>

Peters, Stephen H. and Douglas J. Butler. "A Cost Model for Retrospective Conversion Alternatives." <u>Library Resources and Technical Services</u> 28 (April/June 1984): 149-162.

D101

<u>Abstract</u>: A cost model is presented for use by librarians desiring to investigate various alternatives for accomplishing retrospective conversion. Advice on taking a random sample and gathering information is given, and the steps necessary to cost the project are set out. A hypothetical example using two alternative methods is provided.

Kim, Sook-Hyun. "Southeastern ARL Libraries Cooperative Serials Project Report Phase I: October 1, 1981-December 23, 1982 and Project Manual." 1983. ERIC ED254244. Microfiche.

D102

Abstract: Describes a cooperative serials acquisitions and deselection project for regional resource sharing among eight ARL libraries in the Southeast. Includes statistics for retrospective conversion of cataloging records, the first step in this program, for the University of Tennessee Library at Knoxville.

Johnson, Carolyn A. "Retrospective Conversion of Three Library Collections." Information Technology and Libraries 1 (June 1982): 133-139.

D103

Abstract: Reports the retrospective conversion activities via OCLC of three library collections: a main, a rare-book, and a historical collection. Characteristics that determine the rate of conversion were discussed and conversion rates for each collection compared.

Krieger, Michael T. "Retrospective Conversion at a Two-Year College." Information Technology and Libraries 1 (March 1982): 41-44.

D104

Abstract: Studies the feasibility of an in-house retrospective conversion at a two-year college, using a test file of 350 records.

New York State Library, and others. "Research Library Resources Access Project: Final Report. A Retrospective Conversion Project." 1982. ERIC ED217843. Microfiche.

D105

Abstract: Description of a 3-year retrospective catalog conversion project for monographic records from six major New York State research libraries into machine-readable format using OCLC.

Crismond, Linda F. "Quality Issues in Retrospective Conversion Projects." Library Resources and Technical Services 25 (January/March 1981): 48-55.

D106

Abstract: Reports on a questionnaire sent to 446 members of OCLC to ascertain views on the development of a special minimal standard to be used only for retrospective conversion projects.

Dwyer, James R. "The Effect of Closed Catalogs on Public Access." *Library Resources and Technical Services* 25 (April/June 1981): 186-195.

D107

Abstract: Reports on microcatalog use studies conducted at the University of Oregon; examines user difficulties with multiple-file microfiche catalogs, and compares results to other studies. Retrospective conversion strategies and the costs of converting records into machine-readable form are considered.

Baldwin, Paul E. and Leigh Swain. "RECON Alternatives for Eight British Columbia Public Libraries: An Ancillary Report for the British Columbia Library Network . . . " 1980. ERIC ED200207. Microfiche.

D108

Abstract: Feasibility study to estimate alternative costs in 1980 Canadian dollars of using four bibliographic utilities to accomplish retrospective conversion of the manual card files of eight British Columbia public libraries and to make a recommendation about which to use.

CHAPTER 5

CATALOG STRUCTURE AND USE

GENERAL AND MISCELLANEOUS

E1 Blagden, Pauline. "Women's Studies: An Examination of Library Use by Researchers in the Field with Special Reference to the Fawcett Library." 1985. ERIC ED264894. Microfiche.

Abstract: Questionnaire-based study uses SPSS-X (Statistical Package for the Social Sciences) to compile and analyze responses on library use in women's studies; use of the Fawcett Library (City of London Polytechnic, England); and awareness, use, and evaluation of "BiblioFem," Fawcett Library's catalog.

E2 Kramer, Marilyn. "Compacting a Large Card Catalog." *Library Resources and Technical Services* 29 (July/September 1985): 286-294.

Abstract: This article presents a procedure and formula for compacting a large card catalog quickly and with minimal impact on catalog users.

E3 Papakhian, Arsen R. "The Frequency of Personal Name Headings in the Indiana University Music Library Card Catalogs." *Library Resources and Technical Services* 29 (July/September 1985): 273-285.

Abstract: Previous studies of general library catalogs have found that about two-thirds of the personal name headings occur only once. The card catalogs of the Indiana University Music Library were sampled to see if this observation applied in the case of a special materials catalog.

E4 Aguilar, William. "Influence of the Card Catalog on Circulation in a Small Public Library." *Library Resources and Technical Services* 28 (April/June 1984): 175-184.

Abstract: 198 books were selected randomly from the nonjuvenile collection, and circulation of each title ascertained for a fourteen week period. Subsequently divided into two groups, the catalog records for one group were removed from the catalog, while those for the second group remained intact, and circulation frequency of both groups was compared.

Broadbent, Marianne. "Who Wins? Who Loses? User Success and Failure in the State Library of Victoria." <u>Australian Academic and Research Libraries</u> 15 (June 1984): 65-79.

E5

<u>Abstract</u>: Describes a survey, with structured interviews, of library users. Discusses causes of failure to obtain sought material, including lack of ownership of needed items and difficulty in using the catalogs. Indicates in a general way that the findings have implications for technical services.

Johnson, Karl E. "IEEE Conference Publications in Libraries." <u>Library Resources and Technical Services</u> 28 (October/December 1984): 308-314.

E6

<u>Abstract</u>: Surveys were conducted to determine how libraries handle the conference publications of the Institute of Electrical and Electronics Engineers, the availability of suitable cataloging, and the preference of library patrons regarding access to these publications.

Seal, Alan. "Experiments with Full and Short Entry Catalogues: A Study of Library Needs." <u>Library Resources and Technical Services</u> 27 (April/June 1983): 144-155.

E7

<u>Abstract</u>: Reports on nine projects at the Center for Catalogue Research on the effectiveness of library catalogs with regard to the level of content of entries.

Albrera, Josefa B. "Bibliographic Structure Possibility Set: A Quantitative Approach for Identifying User's Bibliographic Information Needs." <u>Library Resources and Technical Services</u> 26 (January/March 1982): 21-36.

E8

<u>Abstract</u>: Study to determine the bibliographic control requirements of a small to medium-sized public library from the point of view of the expressed needs of the library patron through telephone and catalog reference. Bibliographic elements in addition to author, title, and subject are identified and all elements are measured as to the extent and use of each for retrieval.

Rao, Pal V. "The Relationship Between Card Catalog Access Points and the Recorded Use of Education Books in a University Library." College and Research Libraries 43 (July 1982): 341-345.

E9

Abstract: The report investigates the statistical relationship between the number of card catalog access points provided for a group of randomly selected book titles and the number of times the same titles circulated in a specified period of time.

Welborn, Victoria, Phyllis B. Davis and Saragail Runyon Lynch. "Card Catalog and LCS Users: A Comparison." American Society for Information Science Proceedings 19 (1982): 330-334.

E10

Abstract: Compares library patrons at Ohio State who prefer to use the card catalog with those who prefer the online system. Variables described are sex, age, field of study, class rank, type of training with online systems and previous online experience. Applying chi square analysis, the only significant differences between the two groups were sex and class rank.

Mullikin, Angela G. "The King Research Project: Design for a Library Catalog Cost Model." Library Resources and Technical Services 25 (April/June 1981): 177-185.

E11

Abstract: The Association of Research Libraries sponsored the development of a library catalog cost model. The 72 participating libraries considered alternate forms of catalogs, including various combinations of card, COM, and online, in unified or split forms and prepared input data for computer runs to arrive at costs. Definite conclusions were impossible because of many variables.

Richardson, Valerie L. "Lotka's Law and the Catalogue." Australian Academic and Research Libraries 12 (September 1981): 185-190.

E12

Abstract: Describes a study testing the applicability of Lotka's law to personal author entries in the catalog at State College of Victoria at Frankston and testing W. G. Potter's hypothesis that the proportion of single-incidence authors is higher for smaller libraries than for larger ones.

Seal, Robert A. and others. "Report of the Task Force on Cost Analysis and Technical Considerations." 1979. ERIC ED191473. Microfiche.

E13

Abstract: A study at the University of Virginia Library to determine technical feasibility and costs and to compare costs for several alternatives to the card catalog as part of the project to decide whether to close the Libraries' catalogs in 1981.

McClure, Charles R. "Subject and Added Entries as Access to Information." *Journal of Academic Librarianship* 2 (March 1976): 9-14.

E14

Abstract: Analysis of the number and type of subject and added entries assigned to records in the *National Union Catalog*, *Research in Education*, and *Current Index to Journals in Education*.

Bierman, Kenneth John. "Automated Alternatives to Card Catalogs: The Current State of Planning and Implementation." *Journal of Library Automation* 8 (September 1975): 277-298.

E15

Abstract: Analysis of the state of planning and implementation for computer-based alternatives to the card catalogs in 49 libraries with collections over 250,000 titles and 28 libraries with fewer than 250,000 titles.

CARD CATALOGS

Broadbent, Elaine. "A Study of the Use of the Subject Catalog, Marriott Library, University of Utah." *Cataloging & Classification Quarterly* 4 (Spring 1984): 75-83.

E16

Abstract: Describes a survey of users of the subject catalog of the Marriott Library, University of Utah. By means of a short questionnaire, the survey sought to determine who uses the catalog, for what purposes, and how much information the users seek.

Drone, Jeanette M. "A Use Study of the Card Catalogs in the University of Illinois Music Library." Library Resources and Technical Services 28 (July/September 1984): 253-262.

E17

Abstract: A multifaceted card catalog use study was conducted to determine 1) the hourly rate of use at the sound recording and book/music catalogs, 2) the amount of time users spend at the catalogs, 3) who uses the catalogs and why, 4) what difficulties users encounter, 5) the success rate of users' searches, and 6) recommendations for designing an online catalog.

Golden, Gary A., Susan U. Golden and Rebecca T. Lenzini. "Patron Approaches to Serials: A User Study." College and Research Libraries 43 (January 1982): 22-30.

E18

Abstract: This study, conducted at a separate serial card catalog in a major research library, measures the success of more than four hundred patrons in the bibliographic retrieval of serials.

Hostage, John. "AACR 2, OCLC, and the Card Catalog in the Medium-Sized Library." Library Resources and Technical Services 26 (January/March 1982): 12-30.

E19

Abstract: The impact of AACR 2 on the card catalog in a medium-sized library was analyzed in a study using a random sample from a year's cataloging. Rates of conflict, amount of corrections, and creation of split files were considered under different scenarios.

Packer, Katherine H. and J. Michael Michaud. "The Use and Users of COM Catalogues at the University of Toronto and the Mississauga Library System." Cataloging & Classification Quarterly 3 (Fall 1982): 1-25.

E20

Abstract: Reports on three studies of the use of catalogs at the University of Toronto and the Mississauga Library System: unobtrusive observations of use of fiche and reel COM catalogs; structured interviews at the catalog with users of fiche, reel, and card catalogs; and a timed-search experiment with experienced users in fiche, reel, and card catalogs.

Pease, Sue and Mary Noel Gouke. "Patterns of Use in an Online Catalog and a Card Catalog." College and Research Libraries 43 (July 1982): 279-291.

E21

Abstract: In a study at the Ohio State University, success of patrons in finding titles in two departmental library card catalogs was compared with success in finding the same titles in the online catalog of three and one-half million records. In a later study, the success rate in searching titles of their own choosing in the on-line and card catalogs was measured.

Sage, Charles, Janet Klaas, Helen H. Spalding and Tracey Robinson. "A Queueing Study of Public Catalog Use." College and Research Libraries 42 (July 1981): 317-325.

E22

Abstract: The authors conducted a six-week queueing study of public catalogs in the Iowa State University library system. Data gathered are analyzed primarily to determine if routinely gathered library statistics can validly be used to predict catalog usage.

Hafter, Ruth. "The Performance of Card Catalogs: A Review of Research." Library Research 1 (Fall 1979): 199-222.

E23

Abstract: A review article summarizing catalog use studies, methodology used, results of studies, etc.

Virginia Beach Department of Public Libraries. "Cost/Benefit Analysis of a Catalog system for the Virginia Beach Department of Public Libraries." 1978. ERIC ED153657. Microfiche.

E24

Abstract: This study of the economic feasibility of automating catalog production and maintenance for the Virginia Beach Department of Public Libraries assesses benefits and costs for three alternative approaches: 1) retention of the card catalog; 2) a COM catalog produced within the city; and 3) a COM catalog produced by an outside source.

Bookstein, Abraham. "Effect of Uneven Card Distribution on a Card Catalog." Library Resources and Technical Services 19 (Winter 1975): 19-23.

E25

Abstract: Presents a simple model of catalog growth that allows one to estimate how many drawers will overflow in a period of time.

COM CATALOGS

Adalian, Paul T., Jr., Ilene F. Rockman and Ernest Rodie. "Student Success in Using Microfiche to Find Periodicals." _College and Research Libraries_ 46 (January 1985): 48-54.

E26

Abstract: Report of a user survey to study student usage of a microfiche serials holdings list to determine the accessibility and retrievability of periodical issues housed in four separate locations in the California Polytechnic State University Library.

Hodges, Theodora and Uri Bloch. "Fiche or Film for COM Catalogs: Two Use Tests". _Library Quarterly_ 52 (April 1982): 131-144.

E27

Abstract: Description of an experiment to determine time required to complete a series of multiplication catalog lookup tests.

Packer, Katherine H. and J. Michael Michaud. "The Use and Users of COM Catalogues at the University of Toronto and the Mississauga Library System." _Cataloging & Classification Quarterly_ 3 (Fall 1982): 1-25.

E28

Abstract: Reports on three studies of the use of catalogs at the University of Toronto and the Mississauga Library System: unobtrusive observations of use of fiche and reel COM catalogs; structured interviews at the catalog with users of fiche, reel, and card catalogs; and a timed-search experiment with experienced users in fiche, reel, and card catalogs.

Dwyer, James R. "The Effect of Closed Catalogs on Public Access." _Library Resources and Technical Services_ 25 (April/June 1981): 186-195.

E29

Abstract: Reports on microcatalog use studies conducted at the University of Oregon; examines user difficulties with multiple-file microfiche catalogs, and compares results to other studies. Retrospective conversion strategies and the costs of converting records into machine-readable form are considered.

Borgman, Christine L. and Neal K. Kaske. "On-line Catalogs in the Public Library: A Study to Determine the Number of Terminals Required for Public Access." *American Society for Information Science Proceedings* 17 (1980): 273-275.

E30

Abstract: Provides a basis for determining equipment requirements for public access to an online or microform catalog. A multi-server queueing model is used. The study is based on data from the Dallas Public Library.

Hayes, Robert and Harold Borko. "Using an Online Microfiche Catalog for Technical Service Retrieval of Bibliographical Data." *Information Processing and Management* 16 (1980): 277-289.

E31

Abstract: A prototype system was developed that integrates a microfiche catalog into an online computer system for bibliographic control. This study was undertaken to evaluate the feasibility of such a combined system for operation, technical aspects, and economic competitiveness.

Aveney, Brian and Mary Fisher Ghikas. "Reactions Measured: 600 Users Meet the COM Catalog." *American Libraries* 10 (February 1979): 82-83.

E32

Abstract: A study of COM catalog use at the Los Angeles County Public Library System.

Dwyer, James R. "Public Response to an Academic Library Microcatalog." *Journal of Academic Librarianship* 5 (July 1979): 132-141.

E33

Abstract: Users survey of satisfaction with a COM catalog with consideration of such variables as microfiche use, academic status, and distance from the card catalog.

Force, Ronald W. and Jo Ellen Force. "Access to Alternative Catalogs: A Simulation Model." *College and Research Libraries* 40 (May 1979): 234-239.

E34

Abstract: A computer simulation model was developed to provide the library administrator with information on how many microfilm readers or terminals are necessary for access to COM or on-line catalogs. The decision variables include average patron waiting time, number of patrons lost, and average terminal utilization.

Virginia Beach Department of Public Libraries. "Cost/Benefit Analysis of a Catalog System for the Virginia Beach Department of Public Libraries." 1978. ERIC ED153657. Microfiche.

E35

Abstract: This study of the economic feasibility of automating catalog production and maintenance for the Virginia Beach Department of Public Libraries assesses benefits and costs for three alternative approaches: 1) retention of the card catalog; 2) a COM catalog produced within the city; 3) and a COM catalog produced by an outside source.

DeBruin, Valentina. "Sometimes Dirty Things are Seen on the Screen: A Mini-Evaluation of the COM Microcatalogue at the University of Toronto Library." Journal of Academic Librarianship 3 (November 1977): 256-266.

E36

Abstract: User study of an operational COM catalog to aid in its continued development.

Bourne, Charles P. "Initial Article Filing in Computer-Based Book Catalogs: Techniques, Problems, and Article Frequencies." Journal of Library Automation 8 (September 1975): 221-247.

E37

Abstract: Presents the problem of computer-based filing rules in handling initial articles in many languages. Using a catalog for an academic library collection of approximately 750,000 title entries and over 50,000 initial article entries, an empirical study was made to determine the frequency of misfiling that would occur for each of the 93 articles if simple table look-up procedures were used. Offers suggestions to reduce this error rate.

ONLINE CATALOGS

Bowerman, Roseann and Susan A. Cady. "Government Publications in an Online Catalog: A Feasibility Study." Information Technology and Libraries 3 (December 1984): 331-341.

E38

Abstract: Explores the feasibility of including bibliographic records for US documents in an online public access catalog. Reports the survey results of libraries and related organizations that use GPO MARC records. Compares four methods of obtaining GPO MARC records on the basis of initial costs, recurring costs, and quality.

Clark, Susan M. "Microfiche Readers: A Purchase and Allocation Formula." *Canadian Library Journal* 41 (June 1984): 145-147.

E39

Abstract: Discussion of an allocation formula for microfiche readers in public libraries. The formula, based on a Los Angeles County Public Library study, may be applicable to allocation of online terminals for public access catalogs.

Dickson, Jean. "An Analysis of User Errors in Searching an Online Catalog." *Cataloging & Classification Quarterly* 4 (Spring 1984): 19-38.

E40

Abstract: The study extracts a sample of zero-hit author and title searches from the transaction log of Northwestern University Library's online catalog. It analyzes why the searches failed, in an effort to understand the user's conceptual model of the online catalog.

Drone, Jeanette M. "A Use Study of the Card Catalogs in the University of Illinois Music Library." *Library Resources and Technical Services* 28 (July/September 1984): 253-262.

E41

Abstract: A multifaceted card catalog use study was conducted to determine 1) the hourly rate of use at the sound recording and book/music catalogs, 2) the amount of time users spend at the catalogs, 3) who uses the catalogs and why, 4) what difficulties users encounter, 5) the success rate of users' searches, and 6) recommendations for designing an online catalog.

Matthews, Joseph R. and Gary S. Lawrence. "Further Analysis of the CLR Online Catalog Project." *Information Technology and Libraries* 3 (December 1984): 354-376.

E42

Abstract: Identifies characteristics of uses, tasks, the library setting, and system interface that affects user satisfaction on online catalogs in 31 US libraries.

Shore, Melinda L. "Variation Between Personal Name Headings and Title Page Usage." *Cataloging & Classification Quarterly* 4 (Summer 1984): 1-11.

E43

Abstract: Examines the extent and kind of variation between personal name headings in the catalog and the way author's names are used on title pages in an effort to add to the knowledge required to decide whether authority control in an online environment is needed or justified. The data were tabulated using the MINITAB Statistical package.

Steinberg, David and Paul Metz. "User Response to and Knowledge about an Online Catalog." College and Research Libraries 45 (January 1984): 66-70.

E44

Abstract: Reports on a study of online catalog users of the VTLS system.

Taylor, Arlene G. "Authority Files in Online Catalogs: An Investigation of Their Value." Cataloging & Classification Quarterly 4 (Spring 1984): 1-17.

E45

Abstract: Authority control is discussed from two viewpoints. Data from two research projects that support the need for choosing one form of name are summarized. The author's study of user requests that resulted in no "hits" in an online catalog is described. Data are given to show that for only 6.4% of those requests would our current methods of cross referencing in authority records have been helpful, and that two system programs would have given much assistance.

Thomas, Catherine M. "Authority Control in Manual Versus Online Catalogs: An Examination of 'See' References." Information Technology and Libraries 3 (December 1984): 393-398.

E46

Abstract: Compares two authority control systems in terms of cross references and evaluates the differences as related to the use of online keyword search. Results show that 47% of the cross references made for a manual catalog would not be necessary in an online environment.

Williamson, Nancy J. "Subject-Access in the On-line Environment." Advances in Librarianship 13 (1984): 49-97.

E47

Abstract: A review article which discusses subject access in general and specifically in the on-line public access catalog and the videotex system. Attempts to analyze the problems of providing effective subject access to information as well as examine and synthesize the results of research and investigation.

Broadus, Robert N. "Online Catalogs and Their Users." College and Research Libraries 44 (November 1983): 458-467.

E48

Abstract: A review article on the Council of Library Resources study of online catalogs. The study surveyed twenty-nine libraries to produce data for analysis to support improvement of online catalog system interface features, to improve library implementation and support services for online public access catalogs, and to enable libraries to extend online access services to non-users.

Faulkner, Ronnie W. "User Reaction to The Lambda Online Catalog." Southeastern Librarian 33 (Spring 1983): 6-8.

E49

Abstract: User study of an operational online catalog to aid in its continued development.

Golden, Susan U. and Gary A. Golden. "Access to Periodicals: Search Key Versus Keyword." Information Technology and Libraries 2 (March 1983): 26-32.

E50

Abstract: Study compares searching methods of the Library Computer System (LCS) which uses a fixed length algorithmic search and the Washington Library Network (WLN) which uses a keyword search. One hundred and fifty-two periodicals were searched in both databases to ascertain which method is more effective.

Besant, Larry. "Early Survey Findings: Users of Public Online Catalogs Want Sophisticated Subject Access." American Libraries: 14 (March 1982): 160.

E51

Abstract: Preliminary results of the Online Public Access Catalog Evaluation Project administered by CLR.

Marliw, Michael. "Distribution of Subject Headings in an On-line Academic Library Catalog." American Society for Information Science Proceedings 19 (1982): 186-188.

E52

Abstract: Examines the distribution of subject headings in the online catalog of Ohio State University libraries. Patterns established in this catalog were compared to the OCLC data base and similarities and differences between the two are noted.

Pawley, Carolyn. "Online Access: User Reaction." College and Research Libraries 43 (November 1982): 473-477.
E53

Abstract: Results are reported of a questionnaire administered to users of the University of Guelph Library online circulation system. The online system provides public access to monographs and documents, and the study examines the attitude of users.

Pease, Sue and Mary Noel Gouke. "Patterns of Use in an Online Catalog and a Card Catalog." College and Research Libraries 43 (July 1982): 279-291.
E54

Abstract: In a study at the Ohio State University, success of patrons in finding titles in two departmental library card catalogs was compared with success in finding the same titles in the online catalog of three and one-half million records. In a later study, the success rate in searching titles of their own choosing in the on-line and card catalogs was measured.

Borgman, Christine L. and Neal K. Kaske. "Determining the Number of Terminals Required for an On-line Catalog through Queueing Analysis of Catalog Traffic Data." In Public Access to Library Automation, 1980 Clinic on Library Applications of Data Processing, pp. 20-36. Urbana: University of Illinois Graduate School of Library and Information Science, 1981.
E55

Abstract: Presents method used to estimate the number of terminals needed for an online catalog at Dallas Public Library based on data collected from six locations. Decision tables developed from the data aided in actually determining how many terminals should be placed at each location.

McCallum, Sally H. "Statistics on Headings in the MARC File." Journal of Library Automation 14 (September 1981): 194-201.
E56

Abstract: Library of Congress MARC II files from 1969 through October 1979 were analyzed to gain information on characteristics of headings, expected sizes and growth rates of various subsets of authority files. Study was done to support the Network Development Office of LC in the design requirements of a national authority file.

Moore, Carole Weiss. "User Reactions to Online Catalogs: An Exploratory Study." <u>College and Research Libraries</u> 42 (July 1981): 295-302.

E57

<u>Abstract</u>: In this study, use of four online catalogs was observed. Success-failure rates were compared and user opinions analyzed.

Norden, David J. and Gail Herndon Lawrence. "Public Terminal Use in an Online Catalog: Some Preliminary Results." <u>College and Research Libraries</u> 42 (July 1981): 308-316.

E58

<u>Abstract</u>: The authors have studied the transaction counts from two and one-half years' activity at the public use terminals of the Ohio State University Libraries' prototype online catalog to determine what search options academic library patrons use the most often and whether this pattern varies from that reported in major catalog use studies.

Rastogi, Kunj B. and Ichiko T. Morita. "OCLC Search Key Usage Patterns in a Large Research Library." <u>Journal of Library Automation</u> 14 (June 1981): 90-99.

E59

<u>Abstract</u>: Studies the actual search keys entered by users of the OCLC online system to determine user preference and effectiveness of the preferred search keys.

Borgman, Christine L. and Neal K. Kaske, "On-line Catalogs in the Public Library: A Study to Determine the Number of Terminals Required for Public Access." <u>American Society for Information Science Proceedings</u> 17 (1980): 273-275.

E60

<u>Abstract</u>: Provides a basis for determining equipment requirements for public access to an online or microform catalog. A multi-server queueing model is used. The study is based on data from the Dallas Public Library.

Hayes, Robert and Harold Borko. "Using an Online Microfiche Catalog for Technical Service Retrieval of Bibliographical Data." <u>Information Processing and Management</u> 16 (1980): 277-289.

E61

<u>Abstract</u>: A prototype system was developed that integrates a microfiche catalog into an online computer system for bibliographic control. This study was undertaken to evaluate the feasibility of such a combined system for operation, technical aspects, and economic competitiveness.

Force, Ronald W. and Jo Ellen Force. "Access to Alternative Catalogs: A Simulation Model." College and Research Libraries, 40 (May 1979): 234-239.
E62

    Abstract: A computer simulation model was developed to provide the library administrator with information on how many microfilm readers or terminals are necessary for access to COM or on-line catalogs. The decision variables include average patron waiting time, number of patrons lost, and average terminal utilization.

Matthews, Fred W. "Library Catalogue Automation: Cost-Benefit Factors." 1979. ERIC ED180485. Microfiche.
E63

    Abstract: Description of an automated card catalog system, developed for the Dartmouth Regional Library in Nova Scotia, which uses records of selected fixed-length fields. The costs of operating a system based on MARC-type records and one using selected fixed-length fields are compared.

Williams, Martha E., Stephen W. Barth and Scott E. Preece. "Summary Statistics for Five Years of the MARC Data Base." Journal of Library Automation 12 (December 1979): 314-337.
E64

    Abstract: MARC tapes covering 5 years were analyzed for statistics pertaining to record lengths, field tag occurrences, data element lengths per field tag, and distribution of records by Dewey Decimal Division and the Library of Congress class codes.

Bookstein, Abraham and C. E. Rodriguez. "Performance Test of Hybrid Access Method." Journal of Library Automation 11 (March 1978): 41-46.
E65

    Abstract: Studies a method of accessing online bibliographic information by supplementing truncated search keys with keywords taken from the field of interest.

Bourg, James W., Douglas Lacy, James Lilnas and Edward T. O'Neill. "Developing Corporate Author Search Keys." Journal of Library Automation 11 (June 1978): 106-124.
E66

    Abstract: Investigates the design of procedures derived for the truncated key searches for corporate author records and describes a statistical method for predicting performance of search keys for files of arbitrary size.

Legard, Lawrence K. and Charles P. Bourne. "An Improved Title Word Search
    Key for Large Catalog Files." <u>Journal of Library Automation</u> 9
E67 (December 1976): 318-327.

    <u>Abstract</u>: Using a test database with over 500,000 records, study
    evaluates precision of retrieval of the 3,1,1,1 title search key and
    determines a new search key--4,2,2,2--would provide significant
    improvements in performance.

Williams, Martha E. "Data Element Statistics for the MARC II Data Base."
    <u>Journal of Library Automation</u> 9 (June 1976): 89-100.
E68
    <u>Abstract</u>: Analyzes the statistics of the MARC II database for 1974-75
    showing data element occurrences, lengths, distribution records by
    Dewey Decimal Division and by Library of Congress class codes.

CHAPTER 6

COLLECTION DEVELOPMENT, ANALYSIS AND MANAGEMENT

GENERAL AND MISCELLANEOUS

Bensman, Stephen J. "Journal Collection Management as a Cumulative Advantage Process." <u>College and Research Libraries</u> 46 (January 1985): 13-29.

F1

Abstract: The paper examines the practical implications of the sociobibliometric laws for the management of journal collections in academic libraries.

Millson-Martula, Christopher. "The Effectiveness of Book Selection Agents in a Small Academic Library." <u>College and Research Libraries</u> 46 (November 1985): 504-510.

F2

Abstract: This article describes a study of the relative effectiveness of classroom faculty and librarians as book selection agents in a small academic library.

Broadbent, Marianne. "Who Wins? Who Loses? User Success and Failure in the State Library of Victoria." <u>Australian Academic and Research Libraries</u> 15 (June 1984): 65-79.

F3

Abstract: Describes a survey, with structured interviews, of library users. Discusses causes of failure to obtain sought material, including lack of ownership of needed items and difficulty in using the catalogs. Indicates in a general way that the findings have implications for technical services.

Christensen, John O. "Management of Popular Reading Collections." <u>Collection Management</u> 6 (Fall/Winter 1984): 75-82.

F4

Abstract: Problem of selecting titles for a popular reading collection in an academic library is presented. Method used to analyze the collection is described. A cost analysis of a book rental program and local purchase is presented. Circulation increased steadily as the results of the analysis were instituted.

Roberts, Michael and Kenneth J. Cameron. "A Barometer of 'Unmet Demand': Interlibrary Loans Analysis and Monographic Acquisitions." *Library Acquisitions: Practice and Theory* 8 (1984): 31-42.

F5

Abstract: Monographic interlibrary loan statistics from Dundee University Library are used to furnish evidence that "a considerable proportion of book ILLs consisted of recent, inexpensive in-print items, rarely outside the immediate subject interest of the requesting faculty . . ."

Rutledge, John and Willy Owen. "The Catalog of the Austrian National Library as a Bibliographic Resource for U.S. Libraries." *Library Resources and Technical Services* 28 (October/December 1984): 325-336.

F6

Abstract: The study examines use of the microfiche edition of the catalog of the Austrian National Library by American libraries. This catalog is also compared with other tools, including the *National Union Catalog*.

Serebnick, Judith and John Cullars. "An Analysis of Reviews and Library Holdings of Small Publishers' Books." *Library Resources and Technical Services* 28 (January/March 1984): 4-14.

F7

Abstract: Report on a random sample of 1980 books from *Small Press Record of Books in Print* which were searched for reviews in three indexes and in OCLC for holdings records. The findings suggest that information on the books of small publishers is more readily available than has been assumed.

Calhoun, John and James K. Bracken. "An Index of Publisher Quality for the Academic Library." *College and Research Libraries* 44 (May 1983): 257-259.

F8

Abstract: Reports the construction of a publisher quality index by comparing the number of a publisher's books appearing in *Choice's* "Outstanding Academic Books" list with a publisher's total output.

Hodowanec, George V. "Literature Obsolescence, Dispersion, and Collection
     Development." College and Research Libraries 44 (November 1983):
F9   421-443.

   Abstract: This study determines annual book obsolescence rates for
   individual instructional departments within a university. Analysis of
   such factors as immediacy and intensity of peak usage, use dispersion,
   and the commonality of use have helped to develop an acquisition
   priority weighting formula.

Lewis, David W. "The Use of Journal Access Service and Its Implications
     for Journal Selection at the Center for Research Libraries." 1983.
F10 ERIC ED234810. Microfiche.

   Abstract: Study of journal use at the Center for Research Libraries'
   Journal Access Service. Analysis of use of a sample of 1010 journal
   titles from the 1976/77 Ulrich's International Periodicals Directory
   indicated heavy use of a few titles, 70% English language, and over
   50% in science and technology.

Mason, Thomas R. and Evan Newton. "Forecasting Library Futures:
     Participative Decisionmaking with a Microcomputer Model. Background
F11 Paper. Workshop 3." 1983. ERIC ED238444. Microfiche.

   Abstract: Study describes model microcomputer program for predicting
   collection growth at Cornell University's Olin Library. Tables
   present historical data and predicted growth rate at Olin and 14 other
   Cornell libraries. Conclusions are drawn for projected collection
   size and stack floor area requirements.

Onadiran, G. T. and R. W. Onadiran. "Building Library Collections in
     University Libraries in Nigeria." College and Research Libraries 44
F12 (September 1983): 358-367.

   Abstract: This study, to examine building university library
   collections in Nigeria, reports number of books per student, annual
   growth of library materials, type of selection policy, acquisition
   procedure, and the relationship between book dealers and the
   university libraries.

Williams, Jim and Nancy Romero. "A Comparison of the OCLC Database and New Serial Titles As An Information Resource for Serials." <u>Library Resources and Technical Services</u> 27 (April/June 1983): 188-198.

F13

Abstract: Samples of 200 titles each were drawn from OCLC and NST and each title was searched for a corresponding entry in the other tool. The 217 titles common to both were compared for holdings reports, selected bibliographic data elements, and supplementary notes.

Peters, Andrew. "Evaluating Periodicals." <u>College and Research Libraries</u> 43 (March 1982): 149-151.

F14

Abstract: The Kraft/Polacsek formula to relate and quantify the factors--such as subject relevance, usage, general availability, indexing, cost, format, publisher reputation, and citation frequency--used in evaluating the worth of a journal to a particular collection, are applied at the Central State University Library.

Trubkin, Loene. "Building a Core Collection of Business & Management Periodicals: How Databases Can Help." <u>ONLINE</u> 6 (July 1982): 43-49.

F15

Abstract: Analyzes frequency of citation of core journals in business and management by commercial online bibliographic databases. Lists 83 business and management periodicals each of which is cited in five or more online databases.

Ching-Tat, Lee. "Acquisitions Budget Control in a CAE Library." <u>Australian Academic and Research Libraries</u> 12 (September 1981): 174-184.

F16

Abstract: Presents a formula for distributing book acquisition funds by subject in terms of course areas, student and staff numbers, and average cost per volume. Applies the formula in a technical college library.

Cline, Gloria S. "Application of Bradford's Law to Citation Data." <u>College and Research Libraries</u> 42 (January 1981): 53-61.

F17

Abstract: This study serves as a test of the two formulations of Bradford's law, verbal and graphical, using 5,628 citations to journal literature referenced in <u>College and Research Libraries</u> and <u>Special Libraries</u>, 1940 through 1974. In addition, trends in citation patterns are identified.

Gapen, D. Kaye and Sigrid P. Milner. "Obsolescence." Library Trends 30 (Summer 1981): 107-124.

F18

Abstract: Examines the research done in the area of obsolescence which is defined as the "decline over time in validity or utility of information."

Roberts, H. S. "Profile of a Public Library." New Zealand Libraries 43 (September 1981): 118-120.

F19

Abstract: Describes a method of using statistics from the 1974 New Zealand Census of Libraries to compare public libraries in terms of (1) population of area served, (2) total book stock, (3) circulation, (4) number of full-time staff, and (5) operating expenditure.

Smith, Linda C. "Citation Analysis." Library Trends 30 (Summer 1981): 83-106.

F20

Abstract: An article focusing on the development of citation analysis as a research method, uses and abuses of this method, and prospects for the future. Includes a section on collection development.

Koch, Jean E. and Judith M. Pask. "Working Papers in Academic Business Libraries." College and Research Libraries 41 (November 1980): 517-523.

F21

Abstract: A questionnaire was sent to 119 academic business libraries requesting information on the collection, maintenance, and use of business and economics working papers. For comparison, a sample user survey of the business faculty and graduate teaching assistants of two large midwestern universities was also conducted.

Turner, Stephen J. "Trueswell's Weeding Technique: The Facts." Colleges and Research Libraries 41 (March 1980): 134-138.

F22

Abstract: Recent commentary in library journals concerning Trueswell's "weeding" technique provides a spectrum of opinion. The author feels much of what has appeared in the literature has been in error, and to correct these mistakes he reviews Trueswell's basic method, introduces possible application areas, and addresses a number of popular misconceptions.

Key, Jack D., Katherine J. Sholtz and Charles G. Roland. "The Controlled Circulation Journal in Medicine: Rx or Rogue? Serials Librarian 4 (Fall 1979): 15-23.

F23

Abstract: Survey and evaluation of free medical journals to assess readership and value to the collection in the Mayo Clinic Library.

Kim, Ung Chon. "Participation of Teaching Faculty in Library Book Selection." Collection Management 3 (Winter 1979): 333-352.

F24

Abstract: Importance of teaching faculty members assisting with collection development is discussed. Shows that years of teaching, age, number of graduate courses taught, publication activities, and professional contacts directly relate to the degree of their active participation in collection development.

King, Donald W. "Pricing Policies in Academic Libraries." Library Trends 28 (Summer 1979): 47-62.

F25

Abstract: Discussion of the economics of libraries with emphasis on user charges.

McKenzie, Richard B. "The Economists' Paradigm." Library Trends 28 (Summer 1979): 7-24.

F26

Abstract: Explains the fundamental notions of economic choice and efficiency in the context of a competitive market.

Tsien, Tsuen-Hsuin. "Trends in Collection Building for East Asian Studies in American Libraries." College and Research Libraries 40 (September 1979): 405-415.

F27

Abstract: The history of and trends in, collection development for East Asian materials is traced, along with some comparative data on collection size and growth rate.

"Action Exchange." American Libraries 9 (January 1978): 29 and American Libraries 9 (February 1978): 77.

F28

Abstract: Answers to a question asking the statistical norm for the number of volumes per bibliographic volume and vice versa.

Boyce, Bert R. and Mark Funk. "Bradford's Law and the Selection of High Quality Papers." *Library Resources and Technical Services* 22 (Fall 1978): 390-401.

F29

Abstract: Describes a comparison of the Bradfordian ranking of journals by their production of papers in a subset of the psychological literature, with the same journals ranked by quality of papers as judged by their frequency of citation. The impact of circulation of a journal and its rejection rate on ranking is also considered.

Hirst, Graeme. "Discipline Impact Factors: A Method for Determining Core Journal Lists." *Journal of The American Society for Information Science* 29 (July 1978): 171-172.

F30

Abstract: Describes a method of determining core journals for a discipline using data from the *Journal Citation Reports* to generate discipline impact factors.

Johnson, Carol A. and Richard W. Trueswell. "The Weighted Criteria Statistics Score: An Approach to Journal Selection." *College and Research Libraries* 39 (July 1978): 287-292.

F31

Abstract: A practical and systematic technique for journal selection is presented in terms of a weighted criteria statistic score.

Magrill, Rose Mary and Mona East. "Collection Development in Large University Libraries." *Advances in Librarianship* 8 (1978): 1-54.

F32

Abstract: Review article devoted to recent activities in collection development in large university libraries, with emphasis on research.

Wyllys, Ronald E. "On the Analysis of Growth Rates of Library Collections and Expenditures." *Collection Management* 2 (Summer 1978): 115-128.

F33

Abstract: Discusses a method of determining the average growth rate of a typical library collection. Expenditures also tend to grow exponentially; therefore, analysis of their growth rates is complicated by the effects of inflation. Different methods of compensating for inflation in the analysis are presented.

Baughman, James C. "Toward a Structural Approach to Collection Development." College and Research Libraries 38 (May 1977): 241-248.

F34

Abstract: A method for developing acquisition priorities based upon scholarly need is discussed, using some of the newer techniques in the area of information science. Subject literature behavior and properties are described through the techniques of citation counting, Bradford's law, and Goffman's indirect method.

Broadus, Robert N. "The Applications of Citation Analysis to Library Collection Building." Advances in Librarianship 7 (1977): 299-335.

F35

Abstract: Review article on citation studies for use in the selection process. Citation studies are seen as holding some hope for the improvement of the quality of selection.

Piternick, George. "ARL Statistics--Handle With Care." College and Research Libraries 38 (September 1977): 419-423.

F36

Abstract: The 1975-76 issue of ARL Statistics presents conclusions concerning academic library collection growth. The procedures of drawing these inferences are examined.

Biskup, Peter and Catherine A. Jones. "Of Books, Academics and Librarians: Some Facts about the Book Selection Habits of the Teaching Staff of Two Canberra Institutions of Higher Learning." Australian Academic and Research Libraries 7 (September 1976): 159-170.

F37

Abstract: Summarizes the results of a survey to study (1) the book selection habits of the academic staff of the Australian National University and the Canberra College of Advanced Education and (2) the attitude of these academic staff toward book selection by librarians.

Deprospo, Ernest R. "The Use of Community Analysis in the Measurement Process." Library Trends 24 (January 1976): 557-567.

F38

Abstract: Discussion of the utilization of community data by library decision makers to measure and evaluate library performance.

Drake, Miriam A. "Forecasting Academic Library Growth." College and Research Libraries 37 (January 1976): 53-59.

F39

Abstract: Forecasting techniques developed by government and industry are being applied to various library statistics. These techniques are explained and examples of their use discussed.

Edelman, Hendrik and G. Marvin Tatum, Jr. "The Development of Collections in American University Libraries." College and Research Libraries 37 (May 1976): 222-245.

F40

Abstract: This survey of collection development trends includes comparative growth rates and collection sizes.

Haspers, Jan H. "The Yield Formula and Bradford's Law." Journal of the American Society for Information Science 27 (September-October 1976): 281-287.

F41

Abstract: Expresses the relationship between a number of top producing journals and their cumulative yield in articles and loans in a yield graph. From this a yield formula is deduced; this formula requires 3 constants to fit the observed data while Bradford needs only 2. A method for the estimation of the number of core journals is given.

Leach, Steven. "The Growth Rates of Major Academic Libraries: Rider and Purdue Reviewed." College and Research Libraries 37 (November 1976): 531-542.

F42

Abstract: Following up on Fremont Rider's hypothesis on academic library growth rates, and on the Purdue study of library growth in 1965, this study measures growth rates of the twenty-five largest ARL libraries from 1962-63 through 1973-74, and compares results with Rider and the Purdue study.

Burton, Robert E. "Formula Budgeting: An Example." Special Libraries 66 (February 1975): 61-67.

F43

Abstract: Outlines the development of the Michigan formula for estimating book funds and FTE staffing requirements for academic and research libraries.

DePew, John N. "An Acquisitions Decision Model for Academic Libraries." *Journal of the American Society for Information Science* 26 (July-
F44 August 1975): 237-246.

Abstract: Describes a tentative decision model for book acquisitions that includes weighted inputs and an equation to indicate whether a library should add a title to its collection, refer it to a cooperative group, defer decision, or drop consideration of the title.

Knightly, John J. "Library Collections and Academic Curricula: Quantitative Relationships." *College and Research Libraries* 36 (July
F45 1975): 295-301.

Abstract: This study of twenty-two Texas state-assisted senior college and university library collections analyzes collection "duplication" or "overlap" with respect to common degree programs. Examines the concept that libraries acquire similar book collections in support of similar academic programs.

Line, Maurice B. and Alexander Sandison. "Practical Interpretation of Citation and Library Use Studies." *College and Research Libraries* 36
F46 (September 1975): 393-396.

Abstract: The paper considers the data required to guide (a) the librarian in acquisition (current and retrospective), discarding, and binding; and (b) the information system designer in selecting journals to be scanned for secondary services, selecting items from journals scanned, and retiring items from active files.

Narin, Francis and Mark P. Carpenter. "National Publication and Citation Comparisons." *Journal of the American Society for Information Science*
F47 26 (March-April 1975): 80-93.

Abstract: Using citation and publication data, ranks the United States first in national scientific activity and the Soviet Union a distant second. Describes strengths in various disciplines.

Piternick, Anne B. "Derivation of a Sample of Journal Issues for Tests of Availability and Use." *Journal of the American Society for*
F48 *Information Science* 26 (September-October 1975): 269-270.

Abstract: Describes a method of preparing a sample of journal issues for testing purposes. A computer file was created by listing every issue of a set of journals and random samples were then selected by the computer and printed.

Pope, Andrew. "Bradford's Law and the Periodical Literature of Information Science." *Journal of the American Society for Information Science* 26
F49 (July-August 1975): 207-213.

Abstract: Analyzes journal citations in *A Bibliography on Information Science and Technology* using techniques developed by S. C. Bradford. Isolates 10 core journals.

Skelley, Grant T. "Characteristics of Collections Added to American Research Libraries, 1940-1970: A Preliminary Investigation." *College
F50 and Research Libraries* 36 (January 1975): 52-60.

Abstract: During the years 1940-1970 301 American libraries were reported in *College and Research Libraries* and *College and Research Libraries News* to have added 1454 collections. In this report the collections are analyzed by (1) type of library, (2) type of collection, (3) means acquired, and (4) sources of gifts to academic libraries.

Voigt, Melvin J. "Acquisition Rates in University Libraries." *College and Research Libraries* 36 (July 1975): 263-271.
F51
Abstract: A model for determining acquisition rates for currently published material for universities with extensive doctoral programs is developed. A basic rate is established for the library of a university with a specifically defined program. The rate is then modulated, based on variations in programs from the university as defined.

ANALYSIS OF HOLDINGS

Doll, Carol A. "A Comparison of Children's Collections in Public and Elementary School Libraries." *Collection Management* 7 (Spring 1985):
F52 47-59.

Abstract: Overlap and duplication study of children's collections in two elementary school libraries and in four public libraries in Illinois.

Kelland, John Laurence. "An Evaluation of the Vertebrate Zoology Collection at the R. M. Cooper Library, Clemson University." Collection Management 7 (Spring 1985): 33-45.

F53

Abstract: Statistical analysis of specific subdisciplines in terms of past selection efforts, average copyright dates, circulation frequencies, and numbers of titles in narrow call number ranges.

Loertscher, David. "The Elephant Technique of Collection Development." Collection Management 7 (Fall/Winter 1985): 45-54.

F54

Abstract: Description of a technique of collection development called collection mapping in which the collection segments are charted: the base collection, general emphasis areas, and specific areas. A model technique for building a collection map is presented.

Nisonger, Thomas E. "Editing the RLG Conspectus to Analyze the OCLC Archival Tapes of Seventeen Texas Libraries." Library Resources and Technical Services 29 (October/December 1985): 309-327.

F55

Abstract: In 1984 the academic libraries in the Association for Higher Education of North Texas consortium used the RLG Conspectus to gather data concerning their current collection patterns. OCLC archival tapes were used to generate data for each Conspectus subject group. This paper describes the problems encountered in editing the Conspectus for use in the project and analyzes the Conspectus as a collection evaluation tool.

Payson, Evelyn and Barbara Moore. "Statistical Collection Development Analysis of OCLC MARC Tape Records." Information Technology and Libraries 4 (September 1985): 220-232.

F56

Abstract: Describes how shorter, fixed-length records were extracted from OCLC tapes to produce a variety of management reports.

Shiels, Richard D. and Martha S. Alt. "Library Materials on the History of Christianity at Ohio State University: An Assessment." Collection Management 7 (Summer 1985): 69-81.

F57

Abstract: Presents a collection assessment method utilizing collection comparison to other institutions' collection size, to published bibliographies, and to the Library of Congress.

Thomas, Sarah E. "Collection Development at the Center for Research
	Libraries: Policy and Practice." <u>College and Research Libraries</u> 46
F58 (May 1985): 230-233.

> Abstract: This study finds that a significant number of serials currently received by CRL are also held by twenty or more libraries, as indicated by holding symbols on OCLC and RLIN.

Coutts, Brian E. "Newspaper Preferences of Southern ARL Libraries: A
	Survey." <u>Southeastern Librarian</u> 34 (Fall 1984): 76-78.
F59

> Abstract: Describes a survey to determine current newspaper subscriptions maintained by the Southern members of the Association of Research Libraries.

Doll, Carol A. "A Study of Overlap and Duplication Among Children's
	Collections in Selected Public and Elementary School Libraries."
F60 <u>Library Quarterly</u> 54 (July 1984): 277-289.

> Abstract: Analysis of and methodology for determining collection overlap (two libraries owning the same title) and duplication (one library owns more than one copy of a title) in two elementary school and four public libraries.

Goehner, Donna M. "Core Lists of Periodicals Selected by Faculty
	Reviewers." <u>Technical Services Quarterly</u> 1 (Summer 1984): 17-38.
F61

> Abstract: Tabulates choices made by faculty reviewers at 26 medium-sized academic institutions of periodical titles considered to be basic to libraries supporting work at the master's level. Core titles in each subject category are ranked according to frequency of selection.

Goehner, Donna M. "Periodical Coverage in Academic Collections: A
	Comparison Between Faculty Choices of Core Titles and Holdings of
	Medium-Sized Libraries." <u>Technical Services Quarterly</u> 1 (Summer
F62 1984): 1-16.

> Abstract: Survey analysis comparing subject core periodical lists developed by faculty reviewers against periodical holdings in 26 libraries. Scope of study limited to art, literature, history, psychology, mathematics, and physics periodicals. Results indicate a lack of similarity between periodical titles cited in the faculty core lists and periodical titles available in the libraries surveyed.

Mosher, Paul H. "Quality and Library Collections: New Directions in Research and Practice on Collection Evaluation." *Advances in Librarianship* 13 (1984): 211-238.

F63

Abstract: A review of selective trends in research, methodology, and practice relating to collection evaluation.

O'Connell, John Brian. "Collection Evaluation in a Developing Country: A Mexican Case Study." *Libri* 32 (1984): 44-64.

F64

Abstract: The library collection of the Faculty of Engineering at the University of Quanajuato in Salamanca was examined to determine its degree of utilization and to identify significant factors for judging the value of the collection.

Fasick, Adele M. and John P. Wilkinson. "To Buy or Not to Buy: An Analysis of Some School Library Purchasing." *Canadian Library Journal* 40 (April 1983): 67-73.

F65

Abstract: Report of a survey to determine if American children's magazines were purchased in preference to Canadian children's magazines by Canadian school libraries.

Gwinn, Nancy E. and Paul H. Mosher. "Coordinating Collection Development: the RLG Conspectus." *College and Research Libraries* 44 (March 1983): 128-140.

F66

Abstract: Descriptions of the data gathering process and of the online version of the Conspectus database precede an outline of the benefits, realized and anticipated, to individual institutions.

Lauer, Joseph J. "A Methodology for Estimating the Size of Subject Collections, Using African Studies as an Example." *College and Research Libraries* 44 (September 1983): 380-383.

F67

Abstract: This report provides a formula for estimating the number of Africana titles in large libraries using the Library of Congress classification schedule, and discusses its use for other subjects.

Nesonger, Thomas E. "A Test of Two Citation Checking Techniques for Evaluating Political Science Collections in University Libraries." *Library Resources and Technical Services* 27 (April/June 1983): 163-176.

F68

Abstract: Two techniques that employ citations from journal articles are tested by evaluating university library political science collections. The results of the tests in five libraries are analyzed, as are some of the practical problems in implementing the techniques.

Olaosum, Adebayo. "Materials Provision Survey at the University of Ife Library, Nigeria." *College and Research Libraries* 45 (September 1983): 396-400.

F69

Abstract: Reports on a study to examine the needs of the university's French program, and to assess the adequacy of library resources in meeting the needs.

Potter, William Gray. "Modeling Collection Overlap on a Micro-Computer." *Information Technology and Libraries* 2 (December 1983): 400-407.

F70

Abstract: Shows how an IBM Personal Computer can be used to analyze a large database to determine collection overlap.

Kim, David U. "OCLC-MARC Tapes and Collection Management." *Information Technology and Libraries* 1 (March 1982): 22-27.

F71

Abstract: Discusses the use of OCLC MARC tapes for collection analysis such as counting new titles acquired by subjects, language, and intellectual level.

Miller, Don and Robert T. Dattola. "Methods for Estimating the Number of Relevant Documents in a Collection." *Information Processing and Management* 18 (1982): 179-191.

F72

Abstract: Several statistical sampling methods are evaluated for estimating the total number of relevant documents in a collection for a given query. Simple random sampling, curve fitting and extrapolation, and random sampling with unequal selection probabilities are the three methods investigated. Conclusions are drawn through the use of empirical comparisons.

Moore, Barbara, Tamara J. Miller and Don L. Tolliver. "Title Overlap: A Study of Duplication in the University of Wisconsin System Libraries." *College and Research Libraries* 43 (January 1982): 14-21.

F73

Abstract: Outlines the results of a study of collection overlap for the University of Wisconsin System libraries. OCLC archival tapes provided two years of cataloging data; monograph records created by the cataloging activities of eleven libraries were compared to determine duplication rates.

Penney, Darby. "The Muse in the Stacks: A Survey of Poetry in Public Libraries." *Public Library Quarterly* 3 (Fall 1982): 33-39.

F74

Abstract: Describes an evaluation of the modern American poetry collections in five New York State public libraries.

Saunders, Stewart. "Student Reliance on Faculty Guidance in the Selection of Reading Materials: The Use of Core Collections." *Collection Management* 4 (Winer 1982): 9-23.

F75

Abstract: An analysis of the collection use patterns of the General Library at Purdue University to determine the relative reliability of faculty suggestions and selection tools to meet course-related reading needs of undergraduate students.

Black, George W. "Estimating Collection Size Using the Shelf List in a Science Library." *Journal of Academic Librarianship* 6 (January 1981): 339-341.

F76

Abstract: Describes a methodology utilizing the shelf list as a means of estimating nonperiodical collection size. The results can be used to continue monitoring increases in collection size for the following years.

Goldhor, Herbert. "A Report on An Application of the Inductive Method of Evaluation of Public Library Books." *Libri* 31 (August 1981): 121-129.

F77

Abstract: Discusses the results of a study evaluating a sample of the collection in the St. Andrew Parish Library, Jamaica. Author used the inductive method which consists of taking a sample of titles in a collection and searching them in each of several review journals, book selection tools, and retrospective bibliographies.

Slater, Jack. "Online Collection Statistics: A Comparison of BASIC and SAS." Drexel Library Quarterly 17 (Winter 1981): 61-74.
F78

  Abstract: Description of automated approaches to maintaining collection statistics online in order to provide detailed information about holdings by classification and format.

Strazdon, Maureen E. "A Library Application of the Apple VisiCalc Program." Drexel Library Quarterly 17 (Winter 1981): 75-86.
F79

  Abstract: Brief description of the use of VisiCalc to maintain and manipulate library collection statistics and budget information in a small library.

Townley, Charles T. "Using SPSS to Analyze Book Collection Data." Drexel Library Quarterly 17 (Winter 1981): 87-119.
F80

  Abstract: Description of ways to manipulate selected data on library collections using the procedures available in the Statistical Package for the Social Sciences (SPSS).

Black, George W. "Statistical Determination of Bound Journal Holdings in a Science Library." Serials Librarian 5 (Winter 1980): 31-39.
F81

  Abstract: Discusses a method for determining the number of bound journal volumes in a science library using sampling techniques. Allows the calculation of the extent of both current and non-current titles.

Caudwell, J. and H. S. Roberts. "A Statistical Survey for Automation at Wellington Public Library." New Zealand Libraries 43 (December 1980):
F82 64-65.

  Abstract: Describes a study of samples from the shelflist to obtain estimates needed by developers of an automated circulation system: (1) total number of titles held by the library, (2) total number of copies held by the library, (3) ratio of copies to each title, (4) total number of authors' names, and (5) ratio of authors to titles.

Nisonger, Thomas E. "An In-Depth Collection Evaluation at the University of Manitoba Library: A Test of the Lopez Method." *Library Resources and Technical Services* 24 (Fall 1980): 329-338.

F83

Abstract: A collection evaluation technique that offers a quick and efficient means for obtaining an empirical evaluation of the depth of the collection in specific subject areas was tried on an experimental basis. The technique was tested twice in each of four different subject areas. Although inconsistencies in the results raise questions about the reliability of the technique, further analysis indicates that it does constitute a valid tool.

Burr, Robert L. "Evaluating Library Collections: A Case Study." *Journal of Academic Librarianship* 5 (November 1979): 256-260.

F84

Abstract: Describes a method of evaluating library collections which permits the librarian to asses the adequacy of both the quantity and quality of library resources available to support specific instructional programs.

Davis, Charles H. and Debora Shaw. "Collection Overlap as a Function of Library Size: A Comparison of American and Canadian Public Libraries." *Journal of the American Society for Information Science* 30 (January 1979): 19-24.

F85

Abstract: Study matched random samples of monographs published after 1970 from American and Canadian public libraries with collections of similar libraries of varying size. There is a strong correlation between overlap percentage and the size of the target library, with regression analysis suggesting linearity over a wide range of collection sizes.

Davis, Charles H. and Debora Shaw. "Relative Percentages of Fiction and Non-Fiction in Selected Canadian and American Public Libraries." *Public Library Quarterly* 1 (Summer 1979): 161-167.

F86

Abstract: Discussion of study to measure the relative percentages of fiction and non-fiction in eight American and Canadian public libraries.

Goldhor, Herbert. "US Public Library Adult Non-Fiction Book Collections in the Humanities." Collection Management 3 (Spring 1979): 31-43.

F87

Abstract: Study of the adult non-fiction collection in the humanities held by US public libraries. The purpose is to secure hard data on the extent and quality of these collections. The inductive method of evaluation is used. Sample titles held by one or more libraries are compared with several relevant reviewing journals, book selection tools, or retrospective bibliographies to see if they are listed.

Lupton, David Walker. "Newsstand Magazines and the Public Library." Public Library Quarterly 1 (Spring 1979): 69-79.

F88

Abstract: Survey of sixty three major American public libraries to determine representation in their collections of fifty five leading mass consumer magazines sold on newsstands.

Palmer, Joseph W. "The Availability and Use of Experimental Films." Public Library Quarterly 1 (Winter 1979): 399-414.

F89

Abstract: Describes a study of experimental film availability and use in public library systems in New York State.

Shaw, Debora and Edward A. Stockey. "Contributions of Small Libraries to State-Wide Resource Sharing: A Study of Collection Overlap Through the INCOLSA Processing Center." Public Library Quarterly 1 (Fall 1979): 281-290.

F90

Abstract: An analysis of the INCOLSA Processing Center file to determine public library collection overlap as well as to evaluate the file's utility as a resource sharing tool.

Shaw, Debora and Charles H. Davis. "Cooperative Cataloging and Automated Bibliographic Networks: Consideration for Public Libraries." Public Library Quarterly 1 (Winter 1979): 387-397.

F91

Abstract: Examination of the collection overlap between eight public library collections in the United States and Canada utilizing the OCLC database.

Bolgiano, Christina E. and Mary Kathryn King. "Profiling a Periodicals
    Collection." College and Research Libraries 39 (May 1978): 99-104.
F92

Abstract: Methods for obtaining data about scope, quality, accessibility, and usefulness of existing periodicals collection are presented, including analysis of unmet user needs, comparison with major bibliograhies, analysis of accessibility through abstracts and indexes, and determination of the relationship between the collection and the academic programs it supports.

Gosnell, Charles F. "Obsolescence of Books in College Libraries."
    Collection Management 2 (Summer 1978): 167-182.
F93

Abstract: Originally published in College and Research Libraries 4, March 1944: 115-125. By using techniques of statistical bibliography procedures were established and conclusions drawn about obsolescence rates for general classes of books. Even though the article is 40 years old, it still is relevant for today's library administrators.

Popovich, Charles J. "The Characteristics of a Collection for Research in
    Business/Management." College and Research Libraries 39 (March 1978):
F94   110-117.

Abstract: The citations from dissertations of Ph.D. condidates in the field of business/management were analyzed, focusing on publication form, periodical title, subject, time span, language, and publisher. Information was compared to the holdings of the State University of New York at Buffalo.

Seba, Douglas B. and Beth Forrest. "Using SDI's to Get Primary Journals:
    A New Online Way." ONLINE 2 (January 1978): 10-15.
F95

Abstract: A modified version of Garfield's impact factor formula, incorporating user-determined relevant citation data, is the foundation for an SDI-based journal selection/purchasing model.

Goldstein, Marianne and Joseph Sedransk. "Using a Sample Technique to Describe Characteristics of a Collection." <u>College and Research Libraries</u> 38 (May 1977): 195-202.

F96

Abstract: A sampling procedure is presented which may be employed to identify characteristics of a collection. The technique is applied to Jewish history collections in each of seven university libraries, and comparisons made on the percentage distribution of titles by language and by publication date.

Bryan, Harrison. "Growth Patterns of British and Australian University Libraries." <u>Australian Academic and Research Libraries</u> 7 (June 1976): 100-105.

F97

Abstract: Using published statistics, ranks British and Australian university libraries in terms of book stock and books per full-time-equivalent student.

Darvall, Barbara. "Law Libraries in Australia and Canada: A Note on Two Recent Surveys." <u>Australian Academic and Research Libraries</u> 7 (December 1976): 245-248.

F98

Abstract: Compares the three largest Australian university law libraries and the three largest Canadian university law libraries, using published results of surveys, with an emphasis on monograph and serial holdings.

Cooper, William S., Donald D. Thompson and Kenneth R. Weeks. "The Duplication of Monograph Holdings in the University of California Library System." <u>Library Quarterly</u> 45 (July 1975): 253-274.

F99

Abstract: Presents the results of an investigation of monographic duplication among library collections on the campuses of the University of California.

Lewkowicz, Linda B., Peter L. Oliver and Ronald E. Diener. "Acquisitions Analysis Employing the Statistical Package for the Social Sciences." <u>American Society for Information Science Proceedings</u> 12 (1975): 53-54.

F100

Abstract: Using SPSS the libraries of the Boston Theological Institute have performed various analyses of uniqueness and overlap of their collections. These provide raw data for future cooperative acquisitions and related agreements.

Stewart, Blair. "Periodicals and the Liberal Arts College Library." College and Research Libraries 36 (September 1975): 371-378.

F101

Abstract: Analysis of the periodical holdings of the ten liberal arts college libraries that created the ACM Periodical Bank shows that the "basic list" of periodicals that every such library holds is very short and that these titles are the ones from which the member libraries most frequently requested photocopies.

COLLECTION MANAGEMENT

Broadus, Robert N., "A Proposed Method for Eliminating Titles from Periodical Subscription Lists." College and Research Libraries 46 (January 1985): 30-35.

F102

Abstract: A method is outlined for determining what periodical titles should be reviewed for cancellation by a university library. A list of candidates for elimination is gathered from titles with low citation counts as found in Journal Citation Reports.

Haka, Clifford H. and Nancy Ursery. "Inventory Costs: A Case Study" College and Research Libraries 46 (March 1985): 169-172.

F103

Abstract: Procedures and statistics for a manual inventory and an inventory coordinated with the conversion to an on-line circulation system at the University of Kansas main library are presented.

Line, Maurice B. "Use of Citation data for Periodicals Control in Libraries: A Response to Broadus." College and Research Libraries 46 (January 1985): 36-37. (With response from Broadus, p. 38-39).

F104

Abstract: Response to Broadus' article (College and Research Libraries 46, January 1985) on using low citation-count as a guide to journal cancellations, cautioning careful use of citation counts.

Payson, Evelyn and Barbara Moore. "Statistical Collection Development Analysis of OCLC MARC tape Records." Information Technology and Libraries 4 (September 1985): 220-232.

F105

Abstract: Describes how shorter, fixed-length records were extracted from OCLC tapes to produce a variety of management reports.

Hurt, C. D. "Important Literature Identification in Science: A Critical Review of the Literature." <u>Advances in Librarianship</u> 13 (1984): 239-258.

F106

Abstract: A review article examining methods used to identify important literature in scientific areas with emphasis on the historical and bibliometric approaches.

McCrank, Lawrence J. "Integrating Conservation and Collection Management: An Experimental Workshop Report." <u>Library & Archival Security</u> 6 (Spring 1984): 23-48.

F107

Abstract: An article discussing the implementation of conservation programs in libraries which depend on the use of document examination and diagnostics in initial planning and the integration of conservation into collection management.

Holland, Maurita Peterson. "Machine-Readable Files for Serials Management: An Optimizing Program and Use Data." <u>College and Research Libraries</u> 44 (January 1983): 66-69.

F108

Abstract: The files of data created to support use of a formula to assess serial "value" (reported in <u>College and Research Libraries</u> 37, Nov. 1976) are applied to other kinds of objective serials budget analyses.

Potter, William Gray. "Modeling Collection Overlap on a Micro-Computer." <u>Information Technology and Libraries</u> 2 (December 1983): 400-407.

F109

Abstract: Shows how an IBM Personal Computer can be used to analyze a large database to determine collection overlap.

Turock, Betty J. "Collection Management and Bibliometrics in the Public Library." <u>Public Library Quarterly</u> 3 (Fall 1982): 3-9.

F110

Abstract: Presents a formula which includes availability, status, patterns of use, and core criteria as a measure of the effectiveness of a given collection.

Lawrence, Gary S. "A Cost Model for Storage and Weeding Programs." <u>College and Research Libraries</u> 42 (March 1981): 139-147.

F111

Abstract: The simple mathematical model presented in this paper was developed to analyze the complex cost trade-offs involved in considering storage and weeding to save space. The limitations of the model and the importance of considering non-economic factors in storage and weeding programs are discussed.

Daugherty, Robert Allen. "System Statistics from the Library Computer System (LCS) at the University of Illinois." <u>Library Acquisitions: Practice and Theory</u> 4 (1980): 71-74.

F112

Abstract: Description of the statistical package developed for the University of Illinois' Library Computer System (LCS). Statistics on a library's collection, its use, and its users can help to identify strengths and weaknesses of the collection and can facilitate decision-making in collection development for weeding, ordering duplicates, and ordering new titles.

Kantor, Paul B. "On the Stability of Distributions of the Type Described by Trueswell." <u>College and Research Libraries</u> 41 (November 1980): 514-516.

F113

Abstract: Application of rules for weeding that are based upon the unequal distribution of demand over the collection require that the distribution remain stable over time. A mathematical expression is derived that tests that stability; verification of the expression is not inordinately time consuming and is particularly easy in the case of automated circulation systems.

Nimmer, Ronald J. "Circulation and Collection Patterns at the Ohio State University Libraries, 1973-77." <u>Library Acquisitions: Practice and Theory</u> 4 (1980): 61-70.

F114

Abstract: Report of study analyzing the growth and recorded circulation of a research library's monographic collection for a five-year period, 1973-1977, with anticipated results in the area of collection management information reports.

Schloman, Barbara Frick and Ruth E. Ahl. "Retention Periods for Journals in a Small Academic Library." Special Libraries 70 (September 1979): 377-383.

F115

Abstract: Academic departmental library establishes journal retention schedules based on the responses to a questionnaire aimed at its primary users. As a result of the retention schedules, 19% of the collection was removed to secondary storage, titles were identified for cancellation, and a mechanism was implemented for weeding the shelves.

Weil, S. "Survey on the Use and Cost of Scientific Journals in the Soreq Library." Special Libraries 70 (April 1979): 182-189.

F116

Abstract: Results of a journal use survey conducted at an Israeli research center library to determine whether the budgetary allocation for renewals was justified, and to identify low-use titles which could be cancelled.

Broude, Jeffrey. "Journal Deselection in an Academic Environment: A Comparison of Faculty and Librarian Choices." Serials Librarian 3 (Winter 1978): 147-166.

F117

Abstract: Compares titles chosen by faculty for deselection and those chosen by a generalized deselection model representative of a group of librarians and California State University at Dominguez Hills. Little similarity existed between the two sets of choices but the deselection model was felt to be of value in minimizing the degree of subjectivity in cancellation decisions. The model is described and applied.

O'Neill, Edward T. "The Effect of Demand Level on the Optimal Size of Journal Collections." Collection Management 2 (Fall 1978): 205-216.

F118

Abstract: Presents a model to determine the optimum size of a collection of journals which will minimize the costs of satisfying the requests of library users. Assumes user requests can be satisfied either by journals in the collection or through inter-library loan.

Sinha, Bani K. "Using the Collection-Control Model." *Journal of the American Society for Information Science* 29 (May 1978): 161-163.

F119

    Abstract: Responds to several criticisms of the 1976 model.

Bradford, S. C. "Sources of Information in Specific Subjects." *Collection Management* 1 (Fall/Winter 1976-1977): 95-103.

F120

    Abstract: Much of the literature today concerning user behavioral patterns refers to the Bradford distribution. This is a reprint of the original article that appeared in the British journal *Engineering* in 1934. It explains the method used to arrive at the distribution curve commonly used throughout library literature.

Cayless, C. F. and C. G. Merritt. "The Keeping Cost of Periodicals." *Australian Academic and Research Libraries* 8 (December 1977): 178-185.

F121

    Abstract: Describes a formula for determining the keeping cost of a serial title, (i.e., the cost of getting it into the library and maintaining it, not including subscription cost). The eleven elements of the formula include such things as average annual fixed costs, standard unit times for procedures such as checking and binding, and salary (and overhead) costs per minute of work. The formula focuses on the cost of an individual title, so that differences in keeping cost from title to title may be shown.

Clement, Russell T. "The Duplicate-Replacement System: An Alternative Method of Handling Book Duplicates." 1977. ERIC ED152308. Microfiche.

F122

    Abstract: This report studied the alternative method of using book duplicates as replacement copies for worn or missing stack items. When tested in the Brigham Young University's Lee Library, it cost an estimated $110 and saved over $4,000 for the replacement of 1,000 books.

Turner, Stephen J. "The Identifier Method of Measuring Use as Applied to Modeling the Circulation Use of Books from a University Library." *Journal of the American Society for Information Science* 28 (March 1977): 96-100.

F123

Abstract: Presents a more general identification method than time-since-last-use as an aid in weeding collections. The general theory and a specific case study are presented to indicate the flexibility and practicality of the method.

Wright, Geraldine Murphy. "Current Trends in Periodical Collections." *College and Research Libraries* 38 (May 1977): 234-240.

F124

Abstract: A survey of moderate-sized U. S. academic libraries was conducted to determine current trends in the development and control of periodical collections. Topics covered include selection of new subscriptions, claim procedures, obtaining replacement copies, use of microforms, open versus closed stacks, shelf arrangement, circulation policy, and theft prevention.

Kantor, Paul B. "Availability Analysis." *Journal of the American Society for Information Science* 27 (September/October 1976): 311-319.

F125

Abstract: Expands and applies a recently proposed technique for determining availability of items in a collection; analyzes sources of error and reliability of results. Reports results of a longitudinal study using this technique and applies it retrospectively to a number of previous studies. Implications for library management are discussed.

Maxin, Jacqueline A. "Weeding Journals with Informal Use Statistics." *The De-Acquisitions Librarian* 1 (Summer 1976): 9-11.

F126

Abstract: Describes a small college library journal use study which was begun primarily for evaluating subscriptions and developing commercial binding priorities but also proved useful in weeding. Includes forms used to record and tabulate data.

Sinha, Bani K. and Richard C. Clelland. "Application of a Collection-Control Model for Scientific Libraries." *Journal of the American Society for Information Science* 27 (September/October 1976): 320-328.

F127

Abstract: Proposes a collection control model based jointly on book age and collection proportion in each of several classes. Application to a specific library shows the same number of home uses as occurred in 1968 could have been generated by a collection 60.2% the size of the actual collection. Provides estimates of the number of books to be acquired and weeded.

Windsor, Donald A. "De-Acquisitioning Journals Using Productivity/Cost Rankings." *The De-acquisitions Librarian* 1 (Summer 1976): 1, 8-10.

F128

Abstract: Describes a rank/cost factor study of weeding a journal collection in a small library.

Curtis, Dade T. "A Predictive Model to Cost-Control Older Scientific Materials in Libraries." *American Society for Information Science Proceedings* 12 (1975): 49-50.

F129

Abstract: Deals with the important cost factors present in collections of older scientific titles. These costs can include costs for retention, maintenance, storage, replacement or weeding of journals and books. Describes a predictive model by which a rational policy can be established.

Randall, Gordon E. "Randall's Rationalized Ratios." *Special Libraries* 66 (January 1975): 6-11.

F130

Abstract: Statistics on collection size, acquisitions, and interlibrary loans reported by seventeen IBM technical libraries were used to construct acceptable ratios as follows: acquisitions to total collection size; loans to acquisitions; and budget percentages to be allocated among library materials and staff costs. Ratios suggested for use solely in the industrial library environment.

LOSS RATE

Pinzelik, Barbara P. "Monitoring Book Losses in an Academic Library." *Library & Archival Security* 6 (Winter 1984): 1-12.

F131

   Abstract: Presents a history of various methods of maintaining book loss records used by Purdue University's General Library over the past twenty-five years.

Sutcliffe, Charles. "A Model for the Financial Appraisal of Electronic Book Security Systems with an Application to Berkshire County Libraries." *Library & Archival Security* 6 (Winter 1984): 27-42.

F132

   Abstract: A model for the financial appraisal of book security systems using discounted cash flow methods.

Smith, Frederick E. "Analytical Approaches Used in a Library Security Study." *Library & Archival Security* 5 (Winter 1983): 53-67.

F133

   Abstract: Results of a study which used four approaches in concluding that an electronic security system was needed. The four approaches used were: statistical, monetary, cost-benefit, and non-monetary.

Varner, Carroll. "Journal Mutilation in Academic Libraries." *Library & Archival Security* 5 (Winter 1983): 19-27.

F134

   Abstract: An examination of journal mutilation in academic libraries using the number of replacement pages ordered as a measurement of the amount of mutilation occurring.

Watstein, Sarah Barbara. "Book Mutilation: An Unwelcome By-Product of Electronic Security Systems." *Library & Archival Security* 5 (Spring 1983): 11-33.

F135

   Abstract: Examines the issue and impact of book mutilation as a byproduct of electronic security systems.

Desmarais, Norman. "Losses in a Theological Library." College and Research Libraries 43 (September 1982): 393-395.

F136

    Abstract: A study of the loss rate of St. Mary's Seminary and University Library, Baltimore is reported, and the results compared to the loss rates of other libraries.

Kohl, David F. "High Efficiency Inventoring through Predictive Data." Journal of Academic Librarianship 8 (1982): 82-84.

F137

    Abstract: A study to determine if different subgroups of the collection have substantially different loss and misshelving rates, and, if so, whether the worst problem areas could be predicted from easily obtainable circulation data. Significant predictors of missing materials are described.

Lowry, Glenn R. "A Heuristic Collection Loss Rate Determination Methodology: An Alternative to Shelf-Reading." Collection Management 4 (Spring/Summer 1982): 73-83.

F138

    Abstract: Provides a method for making reliable estimates of collection loss rates with minimal expenditure of resources. Describes the use of sampling techniques to select items and subsequent verification of their presence or absence in the library's collection.

Sleep, Esther L. "Periodical Vandalism: A Chronic Condition?" Canadian Library Journal 39 (February 1982): 39-42.

F139

    Abstract: Analysis to determine the impact of theft and vandalism on service and budget before and after the installation of a security system.

Weiss, Dana. "Book Theft and Book Mutilation in a Large Urban University Library." College and Research Libraries 42 (July 1981): 341-347.

F140

    Abstract: Reports on a questionnaire study of why students in a large urban university steal and mutilate library books and periodicals.

Paris, Janelle A. "School Library Theft." Library & Archival Security 3 (Spring 1980): 29-38.

F141

Abstract: Results of a survey of selected schools in Texas on school library theft.

Romeo, Louis J. "Electronic Theft Detection Systems: A Survey Conducted in 1976: Part 2: University Libraries." Library & Archival Security 3 (Spring 1980): 1-23.

F142

Abstract: Results of a questionnaire answered by 31 university libraries on the use of security systems in those libraries.

Romeo, Louis J. "Electronic Theft Detection Systems: A Survey Conducted in 1976: Part 3: High School Libraries." Library & Archival Security 3 (Summer 1980): 1-16.

F143

Abstract: Results of a survey of electronic theft detection systems in 25 high school libraries.

Romeo, Louis J. "Electronic Theft Detection Systems: A Survey Conducted in 1976: Part 4: Public Libraries." Library & Archival Security 3 (Fall/Winter 1980): 1-22.

F144

Abstract: Reports on electronic security systems in public libraries based on a survey answered by 27 libraries.

Romeo, Louis J. "Electronic Theft Detection Systems: A Survey Conducted in 1976: Part 5: Medical and Law Libraries." Library & Archival Security 3 (Fall/Winter 1980): 99-114.

F145

Abstract: Results of a survey dealing with the impact of electronic theft detection systems in medical and law libraries.

Griffith, J. W. "Library Thefts: A Problem That Won't Go Away." American Libraries 9 (April 1978): 224-227.

F146

Abstract: Discussion of thefts in libraries which includes information on how to figure losses and the feasibility of a detection system.

Michalko, James and Toby Heidtmann. "Evaluating the Effectiveness of an Electronic Security System." <u>College and Research Libraries</u> 39 (July 1978): 263-267.

F147

Abstract: A pre- and post-installation comparison of loss rates is given after installation of an electronic security system. Analysis of costs and benefits and discussion of factors affecting loss rate estimates are presented.

Mott, Sharon. "An Edmonton High School Reduces Book Losses." <u>Canadian Library Journal</u> 35 (February 1978): 45-49.

F148

Abstract: A pilot study initiated by the Edmonton Public School system to report on the relative advantages and disadvantages of the library security system, to document some of the difficulties that might be encountered in introducing it into a high school, and to recommend ways of minimizing these difficulties.

Beach, Allyne and Kaye Gapen. "Library Book Theft: A Case Study." <u>College and Research Libraries</u> 38 (March 1977): 118-128.

F149

Abstract: This article summarizes an investigation of the dimensions, possible motivations, and plausible solutions to book theft in an academic library and is based on an analysis of questionnaires returned by 380 students at Ohio State University.

Miller, Bruce and Marilyn Sorum. "A Two Stage Sampling Procedure for Estimating the Proportion of Lost Books in a Library." <u>Journal of Academic Librarianship</u> 3 (May 1977): 74-80.

F150

Abstract: Description of a two stage methodology for estimating the proportion of lost books in a library collection.

Von Schon, Catherine V. "Inventory 'By Computer'." <u>College and Research Libraries</u> 38 (March 1977): 147-152.

F151

Abstract: A by-product of computerization of the circulation system at the State University of New York at Stony Brook was an inventory of the library collection. With the shelflist as a source, punched cards were produced for each of the volumes in the collection. Results are reported.

Niland, Powell and William H. Kurth, "Estimating Lost Volumes in a University Library Collection." <u>College and Research Libraries</u> 37 (March 1976): 128-136.

F152

    <u>Abstract</u>: This study employed standard sampling theory to make a study of library book losses. With the assumption that the loss was related to the size of the collection each year, thus taking into account the rapid growth in recent years, a rough estimate of the annual loss rate was obtained.

Evans, D. Wyn. "Lost Books." <u>Library Association Record</u> 77 (March 1975): 49-50.

F153

    <u>Abstract</u>: Analysis of book losses in a British university library along with a method for determining the financial impact of those losses.

Kneebone, Ted. "Library Materials that go A.W.O.L. or the Issue of Security in Illinois Academic Libraries." <u>Illinois Libraries</u> 57 (May 1975): 338-343.

F154

    <u>Abstract</u>: Reports the results of a partial inventory of Sangamon State University Library collection and the results of a survey of Illinois academic libraries. The survey was designed to gain more information on such issues as: inventory practices; percentage of loss; use of security systems; and effects of security system installation.

<u>SHELVING</u>

Hubbard, William J. "Sources of Shelving Workload as a Cost Factor in Maintaining Open Stacks." <u>Serials Librarian</u> 8 (Winter 1983): 75-82.

F155

    <u>Abstract</u>: Through examining the source of material shelved at Virginia Polytechnic for one year, the study found that in-house use accounted for 57% of all items shelved, while circulation returns equalled 23% of the shelving load. The degree to which browsing affected the use of the collection is considered in relation to the cost of maintaining open stacks.

Daehn, Ralph M. "The Measurement and Projection of Shelf Space." *Collection Management* 4 (Winter 1982): 25-39.

F156

Abstract: Reviews published literature on the measuring, monitoring, and forecasting shelf space for library collections. Discusses the specific steps necessary to plan and implement a survey of shelf need. It also compares statistical projection with measurement procedures.

Kohl, David F. "High Efficiency Inventorying through Predictive Data." *Journal of Academic Librarianship* 8 (1982): 82-84.

F157

Abstract: A study to determine if different subgroups of the collection have substantially different loss and misshelving rates and, if so, whether the worst problem areas could be predicted from easily obtainable circulation data. Significant predictors of missing materials are described.

Shill, Harold B. "Open Stacks and Library Performance." *College and Research Libraries* 41 (May 1980): 220-226.

F158

Abstract: Using circulation, book availability, and search and library-use statistics, major elements of the direct access debate are tested in a six-year study of a library that has recently undergone the transition from closed to open stacks.

Bennett, Margaret Johnson, David T. Buxton and Ella Capriotti. "Shelf-Reading in a Large, Open-Stack Library." *Journal of Academic Librarianship* 5 (March 1979): 4-8.

F159

Abstract: Discussion of a method of shelf-reading a large collection housed in the open stacks of an academic library. Includes statistical analysis of the results of the completed project.

Cooper, Michael D. and John Wolthausen. "Misplacement of Books on Library Shelves: A Mathematical Model." *Library Quarterly* 47 (January 1977): 43-57.

F160

Abstract: Presents a mathematical model, based on probability theory, to determine the optimal interval for reading the shelves of a library.

USE PATTERNS

Cullars, John. "Characteristics of the Monographic Literature of British and American Literary Studies." <u>College and Research Libraries</u> 46
F161 (November 1985): 511-522.

Abstract: The aim of this study was to determine how scholars use the monographic literature in British and American literary studies and to compare these findings to those of studies involving the journal literature of the humanities.

Line, Maurice B. "Changes in Rank Lists of Serials Over Time: Interlending versus Citation Data." <u>College and Research Libraries</u> 46
F162 (January 1985): 77-79.

Abstract: Reports on British Library Lending Division surveys of its lending patterns, and compares changes in the rankings among the surveys, as well as comparing the rank list of serials requested with rankings from <u>Journal Citation Reports</u>.

Beheshti, Jamshid and Jean M. Tague. "Morse's Markov Model of Book Use Revisited." <u>Journal of the American Society for Information Science</u>
F163 35 (September 1984): 259-267.

Abstract: Tests the basic underlying assumptions of Morse's Markov model of book use, using 11 years of circulation data from a university library. Morse's model fit about 99% of the data for the collection. Contrary to his assumption one of the model's parameters is time dependent.

Fjallbrant, Nancy. "Rationalization of Periodical Holdings: A Case Study at Chalmers University Library. <u>Journal of Academic Librarianship</u> 10
F164 (May 1984): 77-86.

Abstract: A study of the use of periodicals in a medium-sized technological university. Aspects examined were use of individual periodicals in relation to language of publication; patterns of use for interlibrary lending and for multiple copy journals; and methods and costs for acquiring infrequently used periodicals (as gift or exchange publications or by purchase), together with availability from other sources.

Konopasek, Katherine and Nancy Patricia O'Brien. "Undergraduate Periodical
    Usage: A Model of Measurement." Serials Librarian 9 (Winter 1984):
F165 65-74.

Abstract: Reports a simple and practical method for compiling
periodical use in the undergraduate library of the University of
Illinois. The study ranked individual periodical titles according to
their use, identified the status of the user, identified bound volume
use by title and year, and determined loss rate of current issues.
Titles satisfying 90% of patron needs also identified.

Morton, Walter W. "Popular versus Technical Works in the Medical Library:
    A Use Study." Library Resources and Technical Services 28
F166 (July/September 1984): 263-267.

Abstract: A use study was conducted of fifty pairs of popular and
technical monographs in a health sciences library. The books were
matched by subject, date of publication, and date of acquisition.

O'Connell, John Brian. "Collection Evaluation in a Developing Country: A
    Mexican Case Study." Libri 34 (1984): 44-64.
F167

Abstract: The library collection of the Faculty of Engineering at the
University of Quanajuato in Salamanca was examined to determine its
degree of utilization and to identify significant factors for judging
the value of the collection.

Schmitz-Veltin, Gerhard and John J. Boll. "Literature Use as a Measure
    for Funds Allocation." Library Acquisitions: Practice and Theory 8
F168 (1984): 267-274.

Abstract: Discussion of a technique developed by the University of
Constance in West Germany for using past circulation figures as a
major factor in allocating the monographic acquisitions budget among
various subjects. Additional factors covered include the
proportionate purchases made in each subject field during the
preceding three years and the price per volume in each subject field.
Originally published in Zeitschrift fur Bibliothekswesen und
Bibliographie 31 (January/February 1984): 9-17.

Wall, T. "Frequency Distributions of Recorded Use for Students Using
    Academic Library Collections." <u>Collection Management</u> 6 (Fall/Winter
F169 1984): 11-24.

    Abstract: Frequency distributions of recorded use by students are
    presented, modeled, and extrapolated illustrating patterns of uptake
    by potential users. Library use at six institutions was measured
    using mixtures of Poisson distributions with negative binomial
    distributions of means.

Buzzard, Marion L. and Doris E. New. "An Investigation of Collection
    Support for Doctoral Research." <u>College and Research Libraries</u> 44
F170 (November 1983): 469-475.

    Abstract: Citations were analyzed from selected dissertations
    completed at the University of California, Irvine, to determine the
    extent of library support for doctoral research.

Coady, R. P. "Testing for Markov-Chain Properties in the Circulation of
    Humanities Monographs." <u>Collection Management</u> 5 (Fall/Winter 1983):
F171 37-51.

    Abstract: Study attempts to discover if Markov properties exist in
    the circulation of humanities monographs, i.e., how slowly does the
    circulation rate of monographs decline over several years. The
    appendix to the article explains the Markov theory in detail.

Griscom, Richard. "Periodical Use in a University Music Library: A
    Citation Study of Theses and Dissertations Submitted to the Indiana
    University School of Music from 1975-1980." <u>Serials Librarian</u> 7
F172 (Spring 1983): 35-52.

    Abstract: Reports a citation study of bibliographies in music theses
    and dissertations conducted at Indiana University that was carried out
    to measure in-house use of music periodicals. Of the 256 titles
    cited, only 30% were cited more than once. Periodicals in musicology
    had a low rate of obsolescence but those in theory and music education
    had a rate much higher than for the humanities in general.

Lopez, Manuel D. "The Lopez or Citation Technique of In-Depth Collection
    Evaluation Explicated." <u>College and Research Libraries</u> 44 (May 1983):
F173 251-255.

    Abstract: Reports the application of the Lopez citation technique at
    the Dafoe Library, University of Manitoba.

Ross, Johanna. "Observations of Browsing Behavior in an Academic Library." *College and Research Libraries* 44 (July 1983): 269-276.

F174

Abstract: Results of an observational study of user browsing behavior are reported; data include a breakdown of use by LC classification number.

Schmitt, John P. and Stewart Saunders. "An Assessment of *Choice* as a Tool for Selection." *College and Research Libraries* 44 (September 1983): 375-380.

F175

Abstract: A study of the relationship between the strength of the reviews and the subsequent circulation of the titles reviewed. Sampling procedures and results are reported.

Stiffler, Stuart A. "Core Analysis in Collection Management." *Collection Management* 5 (Fall/Winter 1983): 135-149.

F176

Abstract: Study of the circulation of core and non-core titles in a small liberal arts college. Results of a simple application, core and a random sample of non-core approach to collection management showed that the annual circulation of core titles was more than twice the rate of non-core titles.

Bryant, Michelle, Elizabeth McKenzie and Roger Fenton. "Magazines in Stir: A Survey of Periodicals at Arohata Youth Institution, Tawa." *New Zealand Libraries* 43 (December 1982): 205-206.

F177

Abstract: Reports on a survey of the inmates of a women's penal institution about their use of the magazines in the institution's library and their interest in magazines and topics not in the collection. The survey was intended to aid decisions about canceling and adding subscriptions.

Gordon, Martin. "Periodical Use at a Small College Library." *Serials Librarian* 6 (Summer 1982): 63-73.

F178

Abstract: Analyzes observed use of general, humanities, social science and science periodicals in Franklin and Marshall College library. Above 90% of total uses adhered to Bradford's Law of Dispersion. General and social science titles had more uses than humanities titles; and indexing, instruction and housing decisions appeared to increase use of any given title. Other analyses were also made.

Lancaster, F. W. "Evaluating Collections by Their Use." *Collection Management* 4 (Spring/Summer 1982): 15-43.
F179

    Abstract: Presents a theoretical model for evaluating collections in terms of the volume and type of use they are currently receiving and have received in the immediate past. Circulation data serves as the basic source of information.

Moore, Carolyn. "Core Collection Development in a Medium-Sized Public Library." *Library Resources and Technical Services* 26 (January/March **F180** 1982): 37-46.

    Abstract: Reports a procedure built on the research of Trueswell and McGrath, based on the analysis of shelf and circulation samples according to subject, last circulation date, and publication date. Supported by a user questionnaire. Tests whether there will be a difference between fiction and non-fiction, and whether restructuring through weeding and adding titles will have an effect on the circulation-to-heading ratio.

Rao, Pal V. "The Relationship between Card Catalog Access Points and the Recorded Use of Education Books in a University Library." *College and* **F181** *Research Libraries* 43 (July 1982): 341-345.

    Abstract: The report investigates the statistical relationship between the number of card catalog access points provided for a group of randomly selected book titles and the number of times the same titles circulated in a specified period of time.

Saunders, Stewart. "Student Reliance on Faculty Guidance in the Selection of Reading Materials: The Use of Core Collections." *Collection* **F182** *Management* 4 (Winter 1982): 9-23.

    Abstract: An analysis of the collection use patterns of the General Library at Purdue University to determine the relative reliability of faculty suggestions and selection tools to meet course-related reading needs of undergraduate students.

Turock, Betty J. "Collection Management and Bibliometrics in the Public Library." *Public Library Quarterly* 3 (Fall 1982): 3-9.
F183

    Abstract: Presents a formula which includes availability, status, patterns of use, and core criteria as a measure of the effectiveness of a given collection.

Hayes, Robert M. "Application of a Mixture of Poisson Distributions to Data on Use of Library Materials." <u>American Society for Information Science Proceedings</u> 18 (1981): 295-297.

F184

Abstract: Summarizes tests of the hypothesis that a mixture of Poisson distributions can describe and predict distributions of use of library materials by applying such a mixture to 8 independent sets of data presented in the report on the use of library material at the University of Pittsburgh.

Hayes, Robert M. "The Distribution and Use of Library Materials: Analysis of Data from the University of Pittsburgh. <u>Library Research</u> 3 (Fall 1981): 215-60.

F185

Abstract: Evaluation of circulation data as an index of library collection utilization. Studies a mixture of Poisson distribution as predictors of use distribution. Extensive statistical analysis.

Mankin, Carole J. and Jacqueline D. Bastille. "An Analysis of the Difference between Density-of-Use and Raw-Use Ranking of Library Use." <u>Journal of the American Society for Information Science</u> 32 (May 1981): 224-228.

F186

Abstract: Proposes using a "density-of-use rank," obtained by dividing raw-use frequency by the linear feet of shelf space used by the title and then ranking the results for serial collection development decisions. Twice as many titles would be needed to include 80% of the total use of the collection as when ranking by raw use is employed. But fewer feet of shelf space would be needed, cost increases are not great, and the number of potential unsatisfied title uses was reduced.

McCain, Katharine and James E. Bobick. "Patterns of Journal Use in a Departmental Library: A Citation Analysis." <u>Journal of the American Society for Information Science</u> 32 (July 1981): 257-267.

F187

Abstract: Uses citation analysis of faculty publications, doctoral dissertations and doctoral qualifying briefs from a biology department to assess journal use during 1975-77. Examines 60 highly cited titles in detail and looks at citation frequencies of volumes published in 1960-69 and 1970-77. Post-1960 citation frequency for 51 titles is 80% or higher.

Steig, Margaret F. "The Information of Needs of Historians." <u>College and Research Libraries</u> 42 (November 1981): 549-560.

F188

<u>Abstract</u>: Reports the results of a survey of historians in different fields of history. It includes information on the formats from which they get their information, where they find relevant references, an how they use materials in foreign languages. The results are compared with those found in other surveys and with citation studies.

Del Frate, Adelaide A. "Use Statistics: A Planetary View." <u>Library Acquisitions: Practice and Theory</u> 4 (1980): 247-253.

F189

<u>Abstract</u>: Historical statistics from a special library automated circulation system were profiled against the total book holdings to reveal interest patterns and recent changes in use. The analysis resulted in the strengthening of certain subject areas, initiated an automated change detection mechanism; and accelerated the decision to store use history in machine readable shelflist records as a management information system data element.

Hodowanec, George V. "Analysis of Variables Which Help to Predict Book and Periodical Use." <u>Library Acquisitions: Practice & Theory</u> 4 (1980): 75-85.

F190

<u>Abstract</u>: Multiple regression analysis was used to identify the variables which may help explain use of library resources including circulation variables broken down by user groups, the analysis of periodical availability and its effect upon the frequency of periodical use, and the correlation of faculty publication output with the use of books and periodicals.

Kantor, Paul B. "On the Stability of Distributions of the Type Described by Trueswell." <u>College and Research Libraries</u> 41 (November 1980): 514-516.

F191

<u>Abstract</u>: Application of rules for weeding that are based upon the unequal distribution of demand over the collection require that the distribution remain stable over time. A mathematical expression is derived that tests that stability; verification of the expression is not inordinately time consuming and is particularly easy in the case of automated circulation systems.

Kent, Allen, Roger R. Flynn, Jacob Cohen and K. Leon Montgomery. "A Commentary on 'Report on the Study of Library Use at Pitt by Professor Allen Kent et al,' The Senate Library Committee, University of Pittsburgh, July 1969" [i.e. 1979]. <u>Library Acquisitions:</u>
F192 <u>Practice and Theory</u> 4 (1980): 87-89.

> <u>Abstract</u>: Commentary on the "Report on the Kent Study of Library Use" (<u>Library Acquisitions: Practice and Theory</u> 3, 1979: 125-151) by Casimir Borkowski for the Senate Library Committee, University of Pittsburgh.

Nimmer, Ronald J. "Circulation and Collection Patterns at the Ohio State University Libraries 1973-77." (<u>Library Acquisitions: Practice and</u>
F193 <u>Theory</u> 4 (1980): 61-70.

> <u>Abstract</u>: Report of a study analyzing the growth and recorded circulation of a research library's monographic collection for a five-year period, 1973-1977, with anticipated results in the area of collection management information reports.

Pritchard, S. J. "Purchase and Use of Monographs Originally Requested on Interlibrary Loan in a Medical School Library." (<u>Library</u>
F194 <u>Acquisitions: Practice and Theory</u> 4 (1980): 135-139.

> <u>Abstract</u>: Survey of the use pattern of monographs originally requested on ILL. The purpose of the study was to determine whether or not the origin of monographic recommendations could be correlated with their subsequent use as revealed by an analysis of the loan histories recorded on the due date labels.

Shill, Harold B. "Open Stacks and Library Performance." <u>College and Research Libraries</u> 41 (May 1980): 220-226.
F195
> <u>Abstract</u>: Using circulation, book availability, and search and library-use statistics, major elements of the direct access debate are tested in a six-year study of a library that has recently undergone the transition from closed to open stacks.

Wood, Judith B., Julius J. Bremer and Susan A. Saraidaridis. "Measurement of Service at a Public Library." <u>Public Library Quarterly</u> 2 (Summer
F196 1980): 49-57.

> <u>Abstract</u>: A study of volume of use, user activity, and availability of items sought by users in a public library. The measurement techniques used were designed to be carried out by relatively untrained staff or volunteers.

Flynn, Roger R. "The University of Pittsburgh Study of Journal Usage: A Summary Report." <u>Serials Librarian</u> 4 (Fall 1979): 25-33.

F197

<u>Abstract</u>: Presents data on use and costs per use in 6 libraries of the University of Pittsburgh. Results were designed to aid in acquisitions, storage and weeding decisions. The study found that a small percentage of the collections in each library accounted for nearly all the use and that usage was of most recently published volumes.

Goehlert, Robert. "Journal Use per Monetary Unit: A Reanalysis of Use Data." <u>Library Acquistions: Practice and Theory</u> 3 (1979): 91-98.

F198

<u>Abstract</u>: Analysis of retrospective data to examine the number of uses per monetary unit each journal provides. Monetary unit includes the initial ordering cost and the recurring costs of the subscription, accounting procedures, receiving, binding, and storage.

Green, Keith. "An Evaluation of Citation-Return on Reprints." <u>College and Research Libraries</u> 40 (January 1979): 44-45.

F199

<u>Abstract</u>: Reports on a ten-year retrospective study of reprint distribution and their subsequent citation as an indication of use.

Kaske, Neal K. "An Evaluation of Current Collection Utilization Methodologies and Findings." <u>Collection Management</u> 3 (Summer/Fall 1979): 187-199.

F200

<u>Abstract</u>: Evaluates current collection evaluation studies and methodologies. Use of collections can be compared if objectives for the collection are the same. Presents a set of variables to be used in comparative studies. Gives a practical list of possible areas of comparisons with comments.

Maher, William J. and Benjamin F. Shearer. "Undergraduate Use Patterns of Newspapers on Microfilm." <u>College and Research Libraries</u> 40 (May 1979): 254-260.

F201

<u>Abstract</u>: This analysis, based on undergraduate use patterns of newspapers on microfilm at the University of Illinois, presents criteria, such as number of titles, dates requested, and existence of indexes, that should be considered when purchasing microfilmed newspapers.

Maxin, Jacqueline A. "Periodical Use and Collection Development." <u>College and Research Libraries</u> 40 (May 1979): 248-253.

F202

    <u>Abstract</u>: The article gives an example of how use of periodicals in an academic environment has been recorded, how it has been built into a collection development program, and how it has focused on areas for future concern.

McGrath, William E., Donald J. Simon and Evelyn Bullard. "Ethnocentricity and Cross-Disciplinary Circulation." <u>College and Research Libraries</u> 40 (November 1979): 511-518.

F203

    <u>Abstract</u>: Student circulation of books in forty-three major academic disciplines were examined for patterns of disciplinary interdependence. Percentage of books charged out by majors in their own discipline was defined as <u>ethnocentricity</u>; percentage of books in a discipline charged out by non-majors was defined as the <u>supportiveness</u> of that discipline. The correlation between ethnocentricity and supportiveness was examined.

Metz, Paul. "The Use of the General Collection in the Library of Congress." <u>Library Quarterly</u> 49 (October 1979): 415-434.

F204

    <u>Abstract</u>: Study of collection use in the Library of Congress using a comparison of holdings statistics to use data.

Palmer, Joseph W. "The Availability and Use of Experimental Films." <u>Public Library Quarterly</u> 1 (Winter 1979): 399-414.

F205

    <u>Abstract</u>: Describes a study of experimental film availability and use in public library systems in New York State.

Rice, Barbara A. "Science Periodicals Use Study." <u>Serials Librarian</u> 4 (Fall 1979): 35-47.

F206

    <u>Abstract</u>: Two semester study of science periodical use at SUNY at Albany to identify little used titles for storage or discard. Even in a large general collection a small core of titles accounted for a large percentage of use. All science journals were included in the study and results were used to cancel subscriptions and discard volumes.

F207 Sargent, Seymour H. "The Uses and Limitations of Trueswell." College and Research Libraries 40 (September 1979): 416-423. With "A Comment" by Richard W. Trueswell: 424-425.

Abstract: A recent study at Polk Library of the University of Wisconsin-Oshkosh employed Trueswell's statistical method to determine the proportion of little-used materials in the collection. Trueswell's analytical procedures are discussed.

F208 Stenstrom, Patricia and Ruth B. McBride. "Serial Use by Social Science Faculty: A Survey." College and Research Libraries 40 (September 1979): 426-431.

Abstract: The 226 faculty members in the social sciences at the University of Illinois who responded to a survey of their use of serials provided information regarding their serial needs and patterns of use, as well as on the usefulness of specified services.

F209 Wender, Ruth W. "Counting Journal Title Usage in the Health Sciences." Special Libraries 70 (May/June 1979): 219-226.

Abstract: Report of a journal use survey, conducted by the extension division of a university-run health sciences library, that analyzes and compares the interlibrary loan requests of health professionals who receive library services against those health professionals who do not.

F210 Wenger, Charles B., Christine B. Sweet and Helen J. Stiles. "Monograph Evaluation for Acquisitions in a Large Research Library." Journal of the American Society for Information Science 30 (March 1979): 88-92.

Abstract: Presents a computerized method of assisting monograph collection development by correlating circulation with inventory statistics. A circulation/inventory/time or circulation/inventory ratio is used to identify high and low use subject areas. The data can then be used to determine areas in which more or fewer purchases should be made.

F211 Bulick, Stephen. "Book Use as a Bradford-Zipf Phenomenon." College and Research Libraries 39 (May 1978): 215-219.

Abstract: The Bradford distribution is introduced and explained; its ambiguity, arising from two different conceptions, and relationship to the Zipf distribution are discussed. Its application to the interaction between book users and books available for use in a library are discussed.

Healey, James S. and Carolyn M. Cox. "Research and the Reader's Guide: An Investigation into the Research Use of Periodicals Indexed in the Reader's Guide to Periodical Literature." Serials Librarian 3 (Winter 1978): 179-190.

F212

Abstract: Analyzes citations from 25 years of theses and dissertations to ascertain research effectiveness of periodicals indexed in the Reader's Guide. Most titles were not used for research and citations tended to occur within 5 years of publication. Questions the long term retention in hard copy or microfilm of many of these titles.

Hodowanec, George V. "An Acquisition Rate Model for Academic Libraries." College and Research Libraries 39 (November 1978): 439-447.

F213

Abstract: With circulation assumed to imply use and thus need, multiple regression analysis was employed to determine which variables best correlate with circulation. A regression equation recommending a predictive value for the number of books to be added was developed.

Kriz, Harry M. "Subscriptions vs. Books in a Constant Dollar Budget." College and Research Libraries 39 (March 1978): 105-109.

F214

Abstract: Citation analysis was used as an aid in collection development in the field of engineering, to compare the relative usefulness of journals and books to graduate students.

Seba, Douglas B. and Beth Forrest. "Using SDI's to Get Primary Journals: A New Online Way." ONLINE 2 (January 1978): 10-15.

F215

Abstract: A modified version of Garfield's impact factor formula, incorporating user-determined relevant citation data, is the foundation for an SDI-based journal selection/purchasing model.

Shaw, W. M., Jr. "A Practical Journal Usage Technique." College and Research Libraries 39 (November 1978): 479-484.

F216

Abstract: Describes a practical journal usage technique employed at the Case Western Reserve University Libraries. Further study has resulted in a stable division of the collection into components which are used and not used; a technique for rating the relative liability of the unused titles is also provided.

Sinha, Bani K. "Using the Collection-Control Model." *Journal of the American Society for Information Science* 29 (May 1978): 161-163.

F217

    Abstract: Responds to several criticisms of the 1976 model.

Smith, Rita Hoyt and Warner Granade. "User and Library Failures in an Undergraduate Library." *College and Research Libraries* 39 (November 1978): 467-473.

F218

    Abstract: A survey was conducted in the undergraduate library at the University of Tennessee, Knoxville, to determine the availability rate of library materials.

Greene, Robert J. "The Effectiveness of Browsing." *College and Research Libraries* 38 (July 1977): 313-316.

F219

    Abstract: The relationship between the way in which library books are discovered and their subsequent usefulness is examined. The effectiveness of browsing as a method of learning about books is discussed.

Perk, Lawrence J. and Noelle Van Pulis. "Periodical Usage in an Education-Psychology Library." *College and Research Libraries* 38 (July 1977): 304-308.

F220

    Abstract: A study of periodical usage at the Education-Psychology Library, Ohio State University was conducted using the library's closed reserve system for circulation data. Loan period, binding, multiple copies, closed reserve, and indexing services were considered in relation to actual usage.

Saracevic, T., W. M. Shaw, Jr. and P. B. Kantor. "Causes and Dynamics of User Frustration in an Academic Library." *College and Research Libraries* 38 (January 1977): 7-18.

F221

    Abstract: A method of analysis was developed that allows for the calculation of four independent probabilities indicating measures of performance of acquisitions policy, circulation policy, library operations, and users. It is argued that the branching analysis for the combination of effects and the particular measures derived are universally applicable for studying these aspects of library performance.

Turner, Stephen J. "A Formula for Estimating Collection Use." <u>College and Research Libraries</u> 38 (November 1977): 509-513.

F222

> Abstract: A method is presented to estimate the proportion of books in a library which are responsible for the determination of the circulation performance rate of that library; the method is applied to a university library and to a public library.

Wenger, Charles B. and Judith Childress. "Journal Evaluation in a Large Research Library." <u>Journal of the American Society for Information Science</u> 28 (September 1977): 293-299.

F223

> Abstract: Reports on 6-month journal evaluation studies at NOAA libraries in Boulder. Data were collected from a use study, circulation and ILL loan statistics, a core list, local availability, questionnaire returns, subscription costs, and patron input. Results showed a 3-month study would have been sufficient and that titles recommended by scientists has a low probability of low use.

Bulick, Stephen et al. "Use of Library Materials in Terms of Age." <u>Journal of the American Society for Information</u> 27 (May-June 1976): 175-178.

F224

> Abstract: Report of study of monograph use in terms of aging at the University of Pittsburgh. Data covers 5 years of use of materials acquired in 1969, and indicates points at which negligible use can be predicted.

Cushman, Ruth Carol. "Lease Plans--A New Lease on Life for Libraries?" <u>Journal of Academic Librarianship</u> 2 (March 1976): 15-19.

F225

> Abstract: Results of a survey to determine the use of book lease plans in academic libraries and their attendant advantages and disadvantages.

Jenks, George M. "Circulation and Its Relationship to the Book Collection and Academic Departments." <u>College and Research Libraries</u> 37 (March 1976): 145-152.

F226

> Abstract: The computer-produced circulation statistics in the Bucknell University Library for 1973/74 are analyzed by Library of Congress classification and academic department. Comparisons with the number of volumes related to each department and the number of students in the department identify areas of the collection that are underutilized or heavily used.

Kantor, Paul B. "Availability Analysis." *Journal of the American Society for Information Science* 27 (September/October 1976): 311-319.

F227

    Abstract: Expands and applies a recently proposed technique for determining availability of items in a collection; analyzes sources of error and reliability of results. Reports results of a longitudinal study using this technique and applies it retrospectively to a number of previous studies. Implications for library management are discussed.

Maxin, Jacqueline A. "Weeding Journals with Informal Use Statistics." *The De-acquisitions Librarian* 1 (Summer 1976): 9-11.

F228

    Abstract: Describes a small college library journal use study which was begun primarily for evaluating subscriptions and developing commercial binding priorities but also proved useful in weeding. Includes forms used to record and tabulate data.

Sinha, Bani K. and Richard C. Clelland. "Application of a Collection-Control Model for Scientific Libraries." *Journal of the American Society for Information Science* 27 (September/October 1976): 320-328.

F229

    Abstract: Proposes a collection control model based jointly on book age and collection proportion in each of several classes. Application to a specific library shows the same number of home uses as occurred in 1968 could have been generated by a collection 60.2% the size of the actual collection. Provides estimates of the number of books to be acquired and weeded.

Morse, Philip M. and Ching-chih Chen. "Using Circulation Desk Data to Obtain Unbiased Estimates of Book Use." *Library Quarterly* 45 (April 1975): 179-194.

F230

    Abstract: Use of simple probability theory to remove other biases to arrive at estimation of circulation by classification and to predict future circulation.

CHAPTER 7

PRESERVATION/CONSERVATION

GENERAL AND MISCELLANEOUS

Walker, Gay, Jane Greenfield, John Fox and Jeffrey S. Simonoff. "The Yale Survey: A Large-Scale Study of Book Deterioration in the Yale University Library." College and Research Libraries 46 (March 1985):
G1   111-132.

Abstract: Reports on a survey of the physical condition of books and the nature of the collections in the Yale University Library system. Results have been tabulated, compared by computer, and analyzed to provide statistical information.

Williams, Lisa B. "Selecting Rare Books for Physical Conservation: Guidelines for Decision Making." College and Research Libraries 46
G2 (March 1985): 153-159.

Abstract: This article discusses the rationale for, and possible uses of guidelines designed to facilitate conservation decisions by systematically evaluating, quantifying, and weighing such factors as monetary, intellectual, and aesthetic value, projected use, and usability.

McCrank, Lawrence J. "Integrating Conservation and Collection Management: An Experimental Workshop Report." Library & Archival Security 6
G3 (Spring 1984): 23-48.

Abstract: An article discussing the implementation of conservation programs in libraries which depend on the use of document examination and diagnostics in initial planning and the integration of conservation into collection management.

Magrill, Rose Mary and Constance Rinehart. "Selection for Preservation: Service Study." Library Resources and Technical Services 24 (Winter
G4 1980): 44-57.

Abstract: Planning for preservation involves an estimate of the proportion of the collection needing attention. The authors designed a simple rating scale and applied it to a sample of books.

Tomer, Christopher. "Identification, Evaluation, and Selection of Books for Preservation." <u>Collection Management</u> 3 (Spring 1979): 45-54.

G5

    <u>Abstract</u>: Study conducted to establish an objective basis for managerial decisions relating to the preservation of library books. It was concerned with the issues underlying these decisions, focusing specifically upon the problem of accurately and effectively assessing books in terms of their present physical condition and past utility.

Walker, Gay. "Preservation Efforts in Larger U.S. Academic Libraries." <u>College and Research Libraries</u> 36 (January 1975): 39-44.

G6

    <u>Abstract</u>: A survey of preservation activities in large U.S. academic libraries revealed widespread problems of deterioration of library materials.

BINDING

Turner, Stephen J. and Gregory O'Brien. "A Fuzzy Set Theory Approach to Periodical Binding Decisions." <u>Journal of the American Society for Information Science</u> 35 (July 1984): 228-234.

G7

    <u>Abstract</u>: An attempt to apply the fuzzy set theory to the development of a model to aid in bindery decisions. The study tested whether this theory could be applied to a specific collection. Discusses the problems and weaknesses of this kind of application.

Stillings, Craig T. and Fred M. Heath. "Stretching the Bindery Dollar: A Model for Coping with Binding Needs in a No-Growth Library Budget." <u>Southeastern Librarian</u> 32 (Summer/Fall 1982): 45-50.

G8

    <u>Abstract</u>: Model formula to prioritize binding needs based on usage and indexing.

Patterson, Kelly, Carol White and Martha Whittaker. "Thesis Handling in University Libraries." <u>Library Resources and Technical Services</u> 21 (Summer 1977): 274-285.

G9

    <u>Abstract</u>: Libraries of ninety universities granting doctorates were surveyed regarding binding, cataloging, classification, storage, and checking of format practices for theses and dissertations.

REPROGRAPHY

Mikita, Elizabeth G. "Monographs in Microform: Issues in Cataloging and Bibliographic Control." <u>Library Resources and Technical Services</u> 25 (October/December 1981): 352-361.

G10

<u>Abstract</u>: The magnitude of the problem of local bibliographic control of microforms is identified, the history of attitudes and practices regarding the cataloging of microforms is reviewed, and it is suggested that integrated bibliographic access be implemented at local and national levels.

Jarmy, Imre, T. "1978 Library Microfilm Rates." <u>Library Resources and Technical Services</u> 24 (Spring 1980): 164-169.

G11

<u>Abstract</u>: An analysis of rates charged by selected U. S. libraries for producing 35mm. archival quality, silver halide microfilm, with tentative projections of future rates based on current market conditions.

Nitecki, Joseph Z. "Reprographic Services in American Libraries." <u>Library Resources and Technical Services</u> 23 (Fall 1979): 407-421.

G12

<u>Abstract</u>: Evaluation of data gathered in the seventh edition of the <u>Directory of Library Reprographic Services</u> (1978) in terms of the kinds of institutions listed and the types of reprographic services offered. It also reviews some issues of administrative involvement in library reprographic services raised by other studies.

Einhorn, Nathan R. "The Inclusion of the Products of Reprography in the International Exchange of Publications." <u>Library Acquisitions: Practice and Theory</u> 1 (1978): 227-236.

G13

<u>Abstract</u>: A study of the use of reprographic materials in the international exchange of publications.

SHELF PREPARATION

Bierman, Kenneth J. "Unit Time/Cost Study of the Processing Unit, Technical Services Division, Tucson Public Library." Revised edition.
G14 1980. ERIC ED194092. Microfiche.

    Abstract: First of three Technical Services studies to determine unit time and cost estimates for the Processing Unit's activities.

Martin, Barbara and Earl P. Smith. "Materials Processing: Centralized Versus the Individual School, a Continuing Controversy." 1979. ERIC
G15 ED200242. Microfiche.

    Abstract: A two-part survey was conducted in a large school district to determine the kind and extent of centralized versus individual school materials processing with attention focused on long- and short-range implications.

CHAPTER 8

MISCELLANEOUS AND OTHER ARTICLES

Bookstein, Abraham. "Sampling from Card Files." *Library Quarterly* 53 (July 1983): 307-312.

H1

  Abstract: Evaluation of methods for constructing valid samples from card files.

Dowlin, Kenneth E. "The Use of Standard Statistics in an On-line Library Management System." *Public Library Quarterly* 3 (Spring/Summer 1982): 37-46.

H2

  Abstract: General discussion of the types of materials processing and production statistics that can be generated by an integrated automated library system. These can then be used as the basis for a decision support system to provide assistance in daily decision making.

Halperin, Michael. "TPL (Table Producing Language) for Library Reports." *Drexel Library Quarterly* 17 (Winter 1981): 51-60.

H3

  Abstract: Use of TPL to analyze data for interlibrary loan. Principles could be applied to many statistical needs in libraries.

"Update for Statistics Handbook." *American Libraries* 11 (March 1980): 169.

H4

  Abstract: Newsnote stating that ALA's Office for Research will edit and update the National Center for Education Statistics' "Handbook of Standard Terminology for Recording and Reporting Information About Libraries."

Heinritz, Fred J. "Using the Computer for Library Random Sample Selection." *College and Research Libraries* 40 (May 1979): 261-263.

H5

  Abstract: Random sample selection by manual methods is tedious and time-consuming. It is an operation that lends itself well to computerization. A FORTRAN selection program that is appropriate for a wide range of typical library sampling problems is described and made available to the profession.

Rouse, William B. "Tutorial: Mathematical Modeling of Library Systems." *Journal of the American Society for Information Science* 30 (July 1979): 181-192.

H6

Abstract: Discusses purposes of mathematical models and reviews phases of the modeling process including defining performance, representing the problem, predicting performance, estimating parameters, defining an optimization criterion, determining the optimal solution and implementing the results. Presents a selected review of models applied to library problems.

Turner, Stephen J. "Estimating Proportions and Variances." *Collection Management* 2 (Winter 1978): 303-312.

H7

Abstract: This tutorial (4) discusses proportion and variance. Each one of the tutorials builds on the understanding of the previous ones. This article illustrates how confidence intervals for the variance works using tables and formulas. Estimating population proportions is also explained, again using formulas and tables.

Turner, Stephen J. "Estimating the Average Value." *Collection Management* 2 (Summer 1978): 183-189.

H8

Abstract: This tutorial (3) deals with the accuracy of the sample mean estimates. The accuracy of this estimation is dependent on (a) how the sampling is conducted; (b) the size of the sample; (c) confidence in the estimation. Normal distribution, central limit theorem and sample size determination are illustrated in this article.

Turner, Stephen J. "Measures of Dispersion." *Collection Management* 2 (Spring 1978): 59-64.

H9

Abstract: This tutorial (2) shows how different methods of dispersion work. There are three common measures of variability: range, variance, and standard deviation. All three are illustrated with either tables or formulas.

Turner, Stephen J. "Measures of Location." <u>Collection Management</u> (Fall/Winter 1976-1977): 105-113.

H10

<u>Abstract</u>: First in a series of 4 tutorial articles, this tutorial shows how quantitative methods can play an important role in the proper conduct of collection development and management. Although conditions vary considerably in the application of quantative methods, there are three questions addressed in this tutorial:

1. What is the objective of the application?
2. How should the data be collected so that reliable conclusions can be made?
3. What conclusions, with what accuracy and with what confidence, can be properly drawn from the data?

Childers, Thomas. "Statistics That Describe Libraries and Library Service." <u>Advances in Librarianship</u> 5 (1975): 107-122.

H11

<u>Abstract</u>: Review article that looks at statistics used for describing a library unit to the outside world. It is based on a search through library literature on statistics back to 1969 and selectivity into earlier years.

AUTHOR INDEX

Adalian, P. T., Jr.: C1, E26
Agnew, G.: D1
Agulier, W.: E4
Ahl, R. E.: C42, F115
Ahmed, F.: A44, B29
Albrera, J. B.: D15, E8
Alexander, P.: A8, D49
Alison, J.: B71, B115, C88, C102
Allerton, D.: A30, B77
Alper, B. H.: A26
Alt, M. S.: F57
Aluri, R.: D30
Anderson, S. E.: D37
Anker, A. L.: B101, C44
Astle, D.: B67, C86
Aveney, B.: E32
Axford, W. H.: B43, B117

Baldwin, P. E.: B46, D79, D108
Barone, K.: B139
Barth, S. W.: D88, E64
Bastille, J. D.: C32, F186
Baughman, J. C.: F34
Baumann, S.: B126, B129
Baxter, B. A.: A46
Beach, A.: F149
Beheshti, J.: F163
Belanger, C. H.: B80
Bennett, M. J.: F159
Bensman, S. J.: C2, F1
Bently, S.: B59
Besant, L.: E51
Bierman, K.: A34, B11, E15, G14
Bigger, C. J.: B128, C84
Biskup, P.: F37
Black, G. W.: C33, F76, F81
Blagden, P.: E1
Bloch, U.: E27
Bobick, J. E.: F187
Bolgiano, C. E.: C47, F92
Boll, J. J.: B69, F168
Bookstein, A.: E25, E65, H1
Borgman, C. L.: E30, E55, E60
Borko, H.: E31, E61
Borlase, R.: B94
Bourg, J. W.: E66

Bourne, C. P.: D48, E37, E67
Bowerman, R.: D65, E38
Boyce, B. R.: C48, F29
Boyer, Y.: B12
Bracken, J. K.: B5, B130, F8
Braden, S.: D80
Bradford, S. C.: F120
Bremer, J. J.: F196
Britton, H. H.: D80
Broadbent, E.: E16
Broadbent, M.: E5, F3
Broadus, R. N.: B1, B21, C3, E48, F35
Brock, J.: A8, D49
Broude, J.: C49, F117
Brown, N. B.: B66, C85
Bryan, H.: A5, F97
Bryant, M.: C23, F177
Bulick, M.: F211, F224
Bullard, E.: F203
Burgess, S. F.: D16
Burns, L. W.: C75
Burns, R. W.: A9
Burr, R. L.: F84
Burton, R. E.: B118, F43
Busch, B. J.: A12
Butler, B.: A21
Butler, D. J.: D101
Buxton, D. T.: F159
Buzzard, M. L.: F170
Byrum, J. D.: D59

Cameron, K. J.: F5
Capriotti, E.: F159
Carpenter, M. P.: F47
Carterette, R. T.: B78, C25
Caudwell, J.: F82
Cayless, C. F.: A36, C59, F121
Celestre, M.: A32, B9, D27
Charbonneau, G.: C24, D17
Chen, C.: F230
Childers, T.: H11
Childress, J.: C65, F223
Ching-Tat, L.: B81, F16
Christensen, J. O.: F4
Chudamani, K. S.: B6
Clark, S. M.: E39

Clasquin, F. F.: B82, B88, B95, B96, B102, B119, C50, C92, C95, C97, C98, C103
Clelland, R. C.: F127, F229
Clement, R. T.: B22, F122
Cline, G. S.: F17
Coady, R. P.: F171
Cohen, J.: B15, F192
Cohen, J. B.: B88, B120, C95
Cohen, M. S.: B99
Comaromi, J. P.: D40
Cook, C. D.: D51
Cooper, M. D.: F160
Cooper, W. S.: F99
Corey, J. F.: C51, D41
Coutts, B. E.: C8, F59
Covey, C. G.: B93
Cox, C. M.: C52, F212
Coyle, K.: D63
Crismond, L. F.: D106
Crowe, W. J.: D73
Cullars, J.: B3, C4, F7, F161
Curry, D. S.: B42
Curtis, D. T.: F129
Cushman, R. C.: B27, F225

Daehn, R. M.: F1156
Dale, D. C.: D25
Darvall, B.: F98
Dattola, R. T.: F72
Daugherty, R. A.: F112
Davis, C. H.: A15, B47, C76, D69, D86, F85, F86, F91
Davis, M. B.: B140
Davis, P. B.: E10
DeBruin, V.: E36
DeGennaro, R.: B110, C100
Del Frate, A. A.: F189
DePew, J. N.: B30, F44
Deprospo, E. R.: F38
Desmarais, N.: F136
DelVilbiss, M. L.: B44
Dickson, J.: D52, E40
Diener, R. E.: F100
Diodato, L. W.: B50
Diodato, V. P.: B50
Dobrovitz, P.: D64
Dole, W. V.: A30, B34, B77, B132, D26
Doll, C. A.: F52, F60

Dowlin, K. E.: A14, H2
Drake, M. A.: F39
Drone, J. M.: E17, E41
Druschel, J.: D74
Dwyer, J. R.: D107, E29, E33
Dyl, E. A.: B72, C89

East, J. W.: D2
East, M.: F32
Edelman, H.: F40
Eggleton, R.: B57
Einhorn, N. R.: B56, G13
Ejlerson, R.: B55
Elliott, R. W.: A22
Emery, C. D.: B60, C79
Erlandson, J.: B12
Espley, J.: D81
Evans, D. W.: F153

Farrell, D.: B59
Fasick, A. M.: F65
Faulkner, R. W.: E49
Fenton, R.: C23, F177
Finks, L. W.: D57
Fjallbrant, N.: C9, F164
Fleishauer, C.: B103, C53
Flowers, J. L.: B18
Flynn, R. R.: C35, F192, F197
Force, J. E.: E34, E62
Force, R. W.: E34, E62
Forrest, B.: C57, F95, F215
Fox, J.: G1
Fraser, W. C.: B38, B137
Friesner, V. G. F.: B40
Frohmann, B.: D18
Fry, B. M.: B97, C36
Fry, J. W.: A7
Funk, M.: C48, F29

Gallagher-Brown, L.: D63
Gapen, D. K.: D93, F18, F149
Gates, C.: B138
Getchell, S. M. Jr.: B87
Getz, M.: A13, A29
Ghikas, M. F.: E32
Gleaves, E. S.: B78, C25
Godden, I. P.: B39
Goehlert, R.: C37, F198
Goehner, D. M.: C10, C11, F61, F62

Goetz, A.: B139
Gold, S. D.: B121
Golden, G. A.: C26, E18, E50
Golden, S. U.: C26, E18, E50
Goldhor, H.: F77, F87
Goldstein, M.: F96
Gordon, M.: C27, F178
Gosnell, C. F.: F93
Gouke, M. N.: E21, E54
Graham, P. S.: A2
Granade, W.: F218
Grand, J.: B41, B141
Green, K.: F199
Green, P. R.: B133, B136, C17, C31
Greene, R. J.: F219
Greenfield, J.: G1
Gregor, J.: G38, B137
Griffith, J. W.: F146
Griscom, R.: C18, F172
Groot, E. H.: B8
Grosch, A. N.: A23, B49, C77, C78, D97
Gwinn, N. E.: F66

Haka, C. H.: F103
Hall, J. D.: D80
Halperin, M.: H3
Hamaker, C.: B67, C86
Hanson, J. A.: B144
Harris, G.: D3
Haspers, J. H.: F41
Hassell, R. H.: D19
Hayes, R.: E31, E61
Hayes, R. M.: F184, F185
Healey, J. S.: C52, F212
Heath, F. M.: G8
Heidtmann, T.: F147
Heinritz, F. J.: A6, H5
Hendrickson, L.: A32, B9, D27
Hentschke, G. C.: B89, C96
Heroux, M.: B103, C53
Hillman, D.: D67
Hindle, A.: A24
Hirst, G.: F30
Hodges, T.: E27
Hodowanec, G. V.: B19, F9, F190, F213
Holland, M. P.: B73, B116, C19, C68, F108
Horn, J. G.: B61, C80

Horner, W. C.: B108, C99
Hostage, J.: D56, E19
Hubbard, W. J.: F155
Hudson, J.: D75
Huff, W. H.: B28, C69
Huffman, R.: D3
Hulbert, L. A.: B42
Hurt, C. D.: F106

Iehl, R. E.: A3
Ihrig, E.: D23
Irons, R. G.: B52, C29

Jarmy, I. T.: B13, G11
Jenkins, D. L.: D13
Jenks, G. M.: F226
Johnson, C. A.: C54, D103, F31
Johnson, J. J.: D76
Johnson, K. E.: D7, E6
Johnson, M.: D36
Jones, C. A.: F37
Josel, C. S.: D76
Joyce, P.: B62, C81

Kafter, R.: E23
Kantor, P. B.: B25, F113, F125, F191, F221, F227
Kaske, N. K.: E30, E55, E60, F200
Kayner, N. L.: D42
Kazlsuskas, E. J.: A3
Kehoe, E.: B89, C96
Kelland, J. L.: F53
Kelley, J. G.: B52, C29
Kent, A.: F192
Kershner, L. M.: D83
Key, J. D.: C38, F23
Khan, M.: D4
Kim, D. U.: F71
Kim, S.: D102
Kim, U. C.: B145, F24
King, C. B.: B08, C99
King, D. W.: C39, F25
King, M. K.: C47, F92
Klaas, J.: E22
Kline, P. S.: D60
Kneebone, T.: F154
Knightly, J. J.: F45
Knutson, G.: D66
Koch, J. E.: F21

Kohl, D. F.: F137, F157
Kohut, J. J.: B122
Konopasek, K.: C12, F165
Kosa, G. A.: B31
Kovacic, M.: B54
Kramer, M.: E2
Krieger, M. T.: D104
Kriz, H. M.: B104, C55, F214
Kronenfeld, M. R.: B83, C93
Kurth, W. H.: F152

Lacy, D.: E66
Lancaster, F. W.: F179
Landesman, M.: B138
Landram, C.: D1, D91
Lauer, J. J.: F67
Lavellee, L.: B80
Lavigne, J.: B51
Law, D. G.: B14
Lawrence, G. H.: E58
Lawrence, G. S.: E42, F111
Lawton, S. B.: A17
Leach, S.: F42
Leeson, K. W.: B15
Legard, L. K.: E67
Lenzini, R. T.: B61, B63, B68,
    B74, C26, C80, C82, C87,
    C90, E18
Leonhart, T. W.: B37
Leung, S. W.: D68
Lewis, D. W.: C20, F10
Lewkowicz, L. B.: F100
Lilnas, J.: E66
Lincoln, R.: B20, B142
Line, M. B.: B2, C5, C6, C72,
    F42, F104, F162
Loertscher, D.: F54
Lopez, M. D.: F173
Lowell, G. R.: B79, B84, C91, C94
Lowry, G. R.: F138
Lundeen, G. W.: A15, B47,
    C76, D69
Luptin, D. W.: B23, C60, F88
Lynch, S. R.: E10
Lynden, F. C.: B75, B90

Maffeo, S. E.: B10
Magrill, R. M.: F31, G4
Maher, W. J.: A31, B16, F201
Makin, C. J.: C32, F186

Marcum, T. P.: A45
Marliw, M.: D20, E52
Martin, B.: D38, G15
Mason, T. R.: F11
Matthews, F. W.: D84, E63
Matthews, J. R.: D42
Maxfield, M. W.: B40
Maxin, J. A.: C40, C70, F126,
    F202, F228
McBride, R. B.: C43, F208
McCain, K.: F187
McCallum, S. H.: D58, E56
McClure, C. R.: E14
McCrank, L. J.: D8, F107, G3
McCullough, K.: B454
McDonald, D. R.: B40
McDonough, J. G.: D21
McGrath, W. E.: B123, F203
McGregor, J. W.: A37, C61
McHugh, A. L.: A42, B26, C67, D47
McKenzie, E.: C23, F177
McKenzie, M. A.: C62
McKenzie, R. B.: F26
McNellis, C. H.: D5
McPheron, W.: B76
Melby, C. A.: D37
Mendenhall, K.: B7, D22
Merriamn, J. B.: B124, C104
Merritt, C. G.: A36, C59, F121
Merz, T. E.: B62, C81
Messineo, L.: B64
Metz, P.: D81, E44, F204
Meyer, R. W.: D92
Michalko, J.: F147
Michaud, J. M.: E20, E28
Mick, C. K.: A18, A35
Mikita, E. G.: D28, G10
Miller, B.: F150
Miller, B. C.: B48
Miller, D.: F72
Miller, T. J.: F73
Millison-Martula, C.: F2
Milner, S. P.: F18
Montague, E.: A25, A43
Montgomery, K. L.: F192
Moore, B.: D77, F56, F73, F105
Moore, C.: F180
Moore, C. W.: E57
Morita, I. T.: D78, D93, E59
Morse, P. M.: F230

Morton, W. W.: F166
Mosher, P. H.: F63, F66
Mott, S.: F148
Mullikin, A. G.: A33, E11

Narin, F.: F47
Nemchek, L. R.: D29
Nesonger, T. E.: F68
New York State Library: D70, D105
New, D. E.: F170
Newborn, D. E.: B39
Newton, E.: F11
Nichol, W. T.: D6
Niland, P.: F152
Nimmer, R. J.: F114, F193
Nisonger, T. E.: F55, F83
Mitecki, J. Z.: G12
Norden, D. J.: E58

O'Brien, G.: C14, G7
O'Brien, N. P.: C12, F165
O'Connell, J. B.: F64, F167
O'Connor, C. A.: D21
O'Connor, T. A.: D21
O'Neill, E. T.: C56, D30, E66, F118
Olaosum, A.: F69
Oliver, P. L.: F100
Onadiran, G. T.: F12
Onadiran, R. W.: F12
Overmier, J. A.: D23
Owen, W.: D10, F6

Packer, K. H.: E20, E28
Palmer, J. W.: F89, F205
Panetta, R.: D92
Pang, I. S.: D32
Papakhian, A. R.: D50, E3
Paris, J. A.: F141
Pask, J. M.: F21
Paterson, D.: A8, D49
Patterson, K.: D45, G9
Pawley, C.: E53
Payson, E.: F56, F105
Pease, S.: E21, E54
Pejman, M.: D57
Penney, D.: F74
Perelmuter, S.: B41, B141
Perk, L. J.: C63, F220

Perrault, A. H.: B35, B134
Peters, A.: C28, F14
Peters, S. H.: D101
Phelps, D.: A13, A29
Phillips, J.: B66, C85
Pierce, A. R.: D89
Pierce, T. J.: B105
Pinzelik, B. P.: F131
Piternick, A. B.: C73, F48
Piternick, G.: F36
Pope, A.: F49
Popovich, C. J.: F94
Potter, W. G.: D61, F70, F109
Preece, S. E.: D88, E64
Preibish, A.: C13
Price, D. S.: A38
Pritchard, S. J.: F194

Randall, G. E.: B125, F130
Rao, P. V.: E9, F181
Raouf, A.: A44, B29
Raper, D.: A24
Rastogi, K. B.: D78, E59
Reeb, R.: D9
Reid, M. T.: B24, B143, D94
Reidelbach, J. H.: B32, B33, B36, B127, B131, B135
Remmerde, B.: D87
Ricard, R. J., Jr.: D59
Rice, B. A.: C41, F206
Richards, J.: D1
Richardson, V. L.: E12
Rinehart, C.: G4
Roberts, H. S.: F19, F82
Roberts, M.: F5
Robinson, E. J.: A4
Robinson, T.: E22
Rockman, I. F.: C1, E26
Rodie, E.: C1, E26
Rodriguez, C. E.: E65
Rogers, J. V.: D39
Roland, C. G.: C38, F23
Romeo, L. J.: F142, F143, F144, F145
Romero, N.: C22, F13
Ross, J.: F174
Ross, R. M.: A19, A39, D95
Roughton, M.: D33, D82
Rouse, W. B.: A10, H6

Ruschin, S.: B65, C83
Rutledge, J.: D10, F6
Ryans, C. C.: D34, D90

Sage, C.: E22
Sampson, G. S.: B105
Sandison, A.: C72, F46
Saracevic, T.: B25, F221
Saraidaridis, S. A.: F196
Sargent, S. H.: F207
Sauer, T.: B107
Saunders, S.: F75, F175, F182
Schadlich, T.: D35
Schloman, B. F.: C42, F115
Schmitt, J. P.: F175
Schmitz-Veltin, G.: B69, F168
Seal, A.: D14, E7
Seal, R. A.: E13
Seba, D. B.: C57, F95, F215
Sedransk, J.: F96
Serebnick, J.: B3, F7
Shalini, R.: B6
Shaw, D.: D85, F85, F86, F90, F91
Shaw, W. M., Jr.: B25, C58, F216, F221
Shearer, B. F.: B16, F201
Shiels, R. D.: F57
Shill, H. B.: F158, F195
Shirk, G. M.: B32, B33, B36, B127, B131, B135
Shoemaker, T. P.: A20, D96
Sholtz, K. J.: C38, F23
Shore, M. L.: D53, E43
Simon, D. J.: F203
Simonoff, J. S.: G1
Sinha, B. K.: F119, F127, F217, F229
Skelley, G. T.: B58, F50
Slater, J.: F78
Sleep, E. L.: D46, F139
Smith, D.: B70
Smith, E. P.: D38, G15
Smith, F. E.: F133
Smith, L. C.: F20
Smith, R. H.: F218
Snoball, G. J.: B99
Sorum, M.: F150
Southwell, T. B.: A40, B111
Spalding, H. H.: E22
Stecher, G.: D43, D98, D99
Steig, M. F.: F188

Steinberg, D.: E44
Steinbrenner, J.: B100
Stenstrom, P.: C43, F208
Stevens, J. K.: B52, C29
Stewart, B.: A41, C64, C74, F101
Stiffler, S. A.: F176
Stiles, H. J.: B17, F210
Stillings, C. T.: G8
Stockey, E. A.: D85, F90
Stokley, S. L.: B143
Strazdon, M. E.: B85, F79
Sugnet, C.: D67
Sumler, C.: B139
Sutcliffe, C.: F132
Swain, L.: D79, D108
Swanson, R. W.: A27
Sweet, C. B.: B17, F210
Sweetman, P.: B91

Tague, J.: D4, F163
Tatum, G. M., Jr.: F40
Taylor, A. G.: D31, D54, E45
Taylor, J. K.: D89
Taylor, M. R.: D60
Tayyeb, R.: D24
Tenopir, C.: D36
Thomas, C. M.: D55, E46
Thomas, S. E.: C7, F58
Thompson, D. D.: F99
Thompson, J. A.: B83, C93
Thorton, S. A.: B128, C84
Tolliver, D. L.: F73
Tomer, C.: G5
Townley, C. T.: F80
Tracy, J. I.: D87
Trubkin, L.: C30, F15
Trueswell, R. W.: C54, F31
Truett, C.: D11
Tsien, T.: F27
Turner, S. J.: A4, C14, F22, F123, F222, G7, H7, H8, H9, H10
Turock, B. J.: F110, F183
Tuttle, H. W.: A11

University of Melbourne, A1
Ursery, N.: F103

VanPulis, N.: C63, F220
Varner, C.: C21, F134

Virginia Beach Dept of Pub
    Libraries: E24, E35
Vogel, J. T.: C75
Voight, M. J.: F51
Von Schon, C. V.: F151

Wainwright, E.: B112
Walch, D. B.: B86
Waldhart, T. J.: A45
Walker, G.: G1, G6
Walker, J. F.: B122
Walker, V.: D62
Wall, T.: F169
Waltner, N. L.: B108, C99
Wanninger, P.D.: D71
Warner, E. S.: B101, C44
Watson, W.: C15
Watstein, S. B.: F135
Weeks, K. R.: F99
Weil, S.: C45, F116
Weiss, D.: F140
Welborn, V.: E10
Wellisch, H. H.: D44
Welwood, R. J.: B113
Wender, R. W.: C46, F209
Wenger, C. B.: B17, C65, F210, F223
Werking, R. H.: B87
West, M.: A21
West, M. W.: A46
White, C.: D45, G9
White, H. S.: B92, B97, C34, C36
Williams, M. E.: A16,
    D72, D88, D100,
    E64, D68
Williamson, N. J.: E47
Windsor, D. A.: C71, F128
Wittig, G. R.: B114, C101
Wolhausen, J.: F160
Wood, J. B.: F196
Wright, G. M.: C66, F124
Whittaker, M.: D45, G9
Wiedemann, P.: B91
Wilkinson, J. P.: F65
Williams, J.: C22, F13
Williams, J. W.: C16, D12
Williams, L. B.: G2
Wyllys, R. E.: B109, F33

Yu, P. C.: B4, B53
Yunker, J. A.: B93

Zmud, R. W.: A28

SUBJECT/KEYWORD INDEX

Accrual accounting: B99
Acquisitions budget allocation:
    B59, B64, B69, B76, B80, B81,
    B87, B91, B93, B94, B101, B105,
    B106, B113, B119, B121, B122, B123
Acquisitions decision model: B30
Acquisitions priority formula: F9
Acquisitions priorities: F34
Acquisitions rate model: B19
Acquisitions rates: F51
Acquisitions verification: B24
Access points, impact on circulation: E9
African studies collections: F67
American literary studies materials: C4
<u>Anglo-American Cataloging Rules</u>: D59
<u>Anglo-American Cataloging Rules</u>:
    (2nd ed.): D24, D31, D32, D51,
    D56, D57, D60, D61
Architectural drawings collections: D26
Archives: A31, D8
Associated Colleges of the Midwest
    Periodical Bank: A41, C74
Association of Research Libraries (ARL)
    libraries: A2, A12, B37, C8, D1,
    D102
Australian periodical prices: B71, B115
Australian university libraries: B98
Audio-visual cataloging: D39
Audio-visual materials costs:
    B86
Austrian National Library Catalog:
    D10
Availability analysis: F125

BALLOTS: A20, D83, D87, D89
BASIC: F78
Beaver County, Pa. libraries:
    A7
Bibliographic control
    elements: D15
Bibliometrics: F110
Bimodal purchasing model: B94
Biology collections: F187
Biochemistry periodical
    prices: B88

Blackwell North America (BNA):
    D87, D92
Book rental plans: B27, B99,
    F4
Book selection agents: F2,
    F24, F37
Book selection tools: B31
Book deterioration: G1, G6
Book expenditures prediction:
    B107
Book price increases: B43,
    B70, B120
Book price indexes: B43, B80
Boston Theological Institute:
    F100
Bradford's law of dispersion:
    C48, F17, F34, F41, F211
Branching analysis: B25
Brigham Young University: B22
British Columbia libraries:
    D79
British Library Lending
    Division: C5
British literary studies
    materials: C4
British periodical prices: B67
Browsing: F174, F219
Business collections: F21, F94
Business periodicals: C30
Bucknell University: F226

California Polytechnic State
    University: C1
California State University
    at Dominguez Hills: C49
Canadian library automation:
    A17
Card catalog compacting: E2
Case Western Reserve University:
    C58
Catalog cost model: A33
Catalog impact on circulation:
    E4
Catalog searching failures: D52
Catalogers' education: D34

Cataloging backlogs: D1, D21
Cataloging in Publication
 (CIP): B7, D68
Cataloging literature analysis:
 D18
Cataloging quality evaluation:
 D9
Cataloging searching: D21,
 D43
Cataloging staff: D13, D16,
 D80
Cataloguing in Publication
 (Canada): D4
Catholic Subject Headings:
 D6
Center for Catalogue Research:
 D14
Center for Research Libraries:
 C7, C20
Center for Research Libraries'
 Journal Access Service:
 F10
Central State University: C28
Chalmers University: C9
Chemistry periodical prices:
 B96
Chi square analysis: E10
Children's collections: F52,
 F60
Children's periodicals: F65
Choice: B5, B87, F175
Citation analysis: B1, B2,
 B21, B104, C18, C52, F20,
 F34, F68, F94, F170, F187
City of London Polytechnic: E1
Clemson University: F53
Closed catalogs: D107, E13
Collection evaluation: F53,
 F57, F64, F68, F72, F77,
 F83, F84, F94
Collection growth rate: F40,
 F42, F97
Collection growth rate predicting:
 B109, F11, F39
Collection mapping: F54
Collection overlap: D85, F45, F60,
 F70, F73, F85, F99, F100
Collection statistics online: F78,
 F79, F80

Collection size estimation: F67,
 F76
College and Research Libraries:
 F17
Community analysis: F38
Community college libraries: D25
Community college libraries, retro-
 spective conversion: D104
Computerized system pricing: A28
Conference proceedings cataloging:
 D2, D7
CONSER project: D37
Contributed cataloging: D73, D75,
 D90
Core collections: F75, F176, F180
Core periodicals lists: C10, C11,
 C30, C74, F30
Cornell University: F11
Corporate name searching: E66
Corporate names: D51, D60
Council of Library Resources
 On-line Catalog Project:
 E42, E48, E51
Cross references: D54, D55
Current Index to Journals in
 Education: E14

Dallas Public Library: E30,
 E55
Dartmouth Regional Library:
 D84
Decision model: B30
Decision tables: A6
Density-of-use periodical
 ranking: C32
Dewey Decimal Classification:
 D19, D40
Directory of Library
 Reprographic Services:
 G12
Dissertation cataloging: D3
Dissertation processing: D45
Dundee University: F5
Duplicate books: B22
Duplicate exchange lists: B51
Duplicate orders: B20
Duplicates Exchange Union: B57

East Asian studies collections: F27
Eastern Washington University: D87
Edinburgh University Library: B14
Education collections: C63, E9
Eighteenth Century Short Title
    Catalogue: D23
Electronic book security systems:
    F132, F142, F143, F144, F145,
    F147
Engineering journals: B104
Error rate in catalogs: D48
Error reports to OCLC: D76
Ethnocentricity in book use: F203
Experimental films: F89

Faculty as book selectors: F2,
    F24, F37, F75
Faculty as journal selectors: C11
Fiction collection size: F86
Film collections: F89
Fine arts acquisitions: B34
Fixed length records: D84
Formula budgeting: B118
Franklin and Marshall College: C27
Free periodicals: C38
Fuzzy set theory: A4, C14

Garfield's impact factor formula:
    C57
Gift evaluation: B50
Goffman's indirect method:
    F34
Government publications:
    D65

Historical collections, retro-
    spective conversion:
    D103
Historical literature: F188
History of Christianity collec-
    tions: F57
Health sciences libraries: B42
Health sciences periodicals:
    C46
Humanities collections: F87,
    F171

IEEE publications: D7
INCOLSA Processing Center: D85

Information science periodicals:
    F49
Indiana University: C18, D50,
    D73
Initial article filing: E37
Interlibrary loan and book acqui-
    sitions: F5
Inventoring: F103, F137, F151,
    F154
Invoice payment: B10
Iowa State University: E22
ISSN: D46

Jewish history collections: F96
Journal Citation Reports: F30

Keyword searching: E50, E65
King Research project: A33
Kiviat-graphs: A22
Kraft-Polacsek formula: C28

Lambda online catalog: E49
Law libraries: F98
Liberal arts colleges periodicals:
    C74
Library Computer System (LCS): E50,
    F112
Library management system statis-
    tics: A14
Library of Congress: F204
Literature obsolescence: F9, F18,
    F93
Lopez method: F83, F173
Los Angeles County Public Library:
    E32
Lotka's law: D61, E12
Louisiana State University: B143

Management periodicals: C30
MARC Records: A16, D58,
    D68, D72, D88, D100
Markov-chain properties: F17
Mass market periodicals: F88
Mathematical models: H6
Mayo Clinic: C38
Medical collections: F166
Medical library cataloging:
    D23
Medical libraries: F194

Medical periodicals: B102, C38
Microcomputer applications: F11, F70, F79
Microcompuers in serials management: C75
Microfilm charges by libraries: B13
Microfilm use: B16
Microform cataloging: D28
Microform reader allocation formula: E34, E39
Microform serials: B78
MINITAB statistical package: D5, D53
Misshelving rates: F137
Mississauga Library System: E20
Molecular biology periodical prices: B88
Monograph evaluation: B17
Monograph literature use: C4
Monograph vendors: B126, B129, B138, B139, B140, B142, B143, B144, B145
Monograph verification: B8
Morse's Markov model of book use: F163
Multiple regression analysis: B19
Multi-server queueing model: E30
Municipal reference library: D66
Music classification: B19
Music collection catalogs: D50, E17
Music collections: C18
Music periodical use: C18
Mutilation of books: F135, F140
Mutilation of journals: C21, F139

Name added entries: E14
National Library of China: B4
National Union Catalog: C16, E14
New England Serials Service: C62
New Serial Titles: C22
New Zealand libraries: A8, F19
Newspaper subscriptions: C8
Newspapers on microfilm use: B16
Newsstand magazines: F88
Nigerian libraries: F12
Nonprint cataloging: D39

Nonprint media price index: B86
Non-Roman script cataloging: D44
Northwestern University: D52

OCLC: B24, C51
OCLC catalog cards: D36
OCLC database: C16, C22, D20, D21, D30, D33, D37, D66, D71, D73, D75, D76, D77, D81, D82, D87, D89, D90, D91, D92, D99
OCLC tapes and management reports: F56, F71
Ohio State University: D20, D93, E10, E21, E58, F57, F114, F149
Open stacks: F158, F159

Part-time work: A1
Periodical accessibility: D1
Periodical collection management: B110, C2, C66
Periodical collection size: C56
Periodical collection size estimates: C33
Periodical collections: D47
Periodical evaluation: C28
Periodical issues circulation: C15
Periodical lending patterns: C5
Periodical maintenance costs: A36
Periodical price increase analysis: B83, B88, B96, B110, B119
Periodical price indexes: B61, B63, B66, B68, B71, B74, B79, B80, B82, B84, B95, B108, B124
Periodical retention schedules: C42
Periodical selection: C54, C57, C65, C72
Periodical subscription cancellation: B1, B2, B92, B97, B103, B116, C3, C6, C34, C36, C41, C42, C49, C70, C71, C72
Periodical subscription costs model: B60, B119
Periodical subscription rate differences: B62, B65, B67, B72, B114

Periodical title changes: C24
Periodical three year subscriptions: B89
Periodical use: C12, C18, C20, C23, C27, C32, C35, C37, C40, C41, C43, C45, C46, C52, C58, C63, C65
Periodical use studies: C70, C72
Personal name headings: D50, D53, D60, D61, E12
Physics periodical prices: B96
PLAN project: A20
Poetry collections: F74
Poisson distributions: F169, F184, F185
Political science collections: F68
Popular monographs: F166
Popular reading collections: F4
Price discrimination in periodicals: B62, B65, B67, B72, B114
Price-movement index: A40, B112
Prison libraries: C23
Psychology collections: C63
Psychology periodicals: C48
Publisher quality index: B5
Purdue University: F75, F131

Queueing study: E22

Random sampling: D101
Rare book cataloging: D8, D23
Rare book collections: G2
Rare book collections, retrospective conversion: D103
Ratios in technical services: B125
Reader's Guide to Periodical Literature: C52
Record matching: D63
Replacement copies: B22
Reprints: F199
Reproductions, cataloging: D5
Research in Education: E14, D61, E12
Resource allocation: A10
RLG conspectus: F55, F66
RLIN (Research Libraries Information Network): D67

St. Andrew Parish Library (Jamaica): F77
Sample selection: C73, H1, H5
Sandusky Public Library: B100
School libraries: A32, F65, F141, F149
School libraries, cataloging: D11, D38, D39
Science acquisitions: B120
Science collections: F76, F106, F119, F127, F129
Science periodicals: C41
Search key searching: E50, E65, E66, E67
Search keys: D78
Sequential analysis: B40
Serials budget: B73
Serials catalog use: C26
Serials cataloging: D37
Serials catalogs: E18
Serials department staffing: A37
Serials holdings list: C1, E26
Serials issue receipt prediction: C78
Serials payment records: B23
Serials processing: C51
Serials records: D82
Serials vendors: B28, B128, B133, B136
Shelf list: F76, F82
Shelf reading: F159, F160
Short entry cataloging: D14
Small press publications: B3
Social science periodicals: C43
Sociobibliometric laws: C2
Soviet serials exchanges: B52
Special Libraries: F17
Staff reorganization: A12
Standing order cancellation: C53
Standing orders: B103
Stanford University: B51
State College of Victoria at Frankston (Australia): E12
State documents acquisition: B12

State Library of Victoria (Australia): E5
State University of New York at Albany: C41
State University of New York at Buffalo: F94
Statistical Analysis System (SAS): D68, F78
Statistical methods tutorial: H7, H8, H9, H10
Statistical Pacage for the Social Sciences (SPSS): A3, D8, E1, F80, F100
Subject access: E47, E51
Subject added entries: E14
Subject catalog: E16
Subject headings: D20, D30, D35, D62
Subject lists of core periodicals: B102
Subject specialists: B31

Table Producing Language (TPL): H3
Taylor's Constant: C24
Technical monographs: F166
Terminal allocation formula: E30, E34, E39, E55
Theater collections: D29
Theological collections: F136
Theological subject headings: D6
Theses cataloging: D3, D45
Theses processing: D45
Time logs: B18
Title word searching: E67
Trueswell's distribution: F22, F113, F207
Tucson Public Library: A34, B11, D42

Undergraduate libraries: F218
Undergraduate materials: F75
Undergraduate periodical use: C12
Undergraduate use of microfilm: B16
<u>Union List of Serials</u>: C16
Universidad de Guanajuato: F64
University of British Columbia: C15
University of California: B70

University of California, Irvine: C170
University of California System: F99
University of California union catalog: D48, D63
University of Constance (West Germany): B69
University of Denver: B144
University of Guelph: E53
University of Ife (Nigeria): F69
University of Illinois at Urbana-Champaign: A31, B16, C12, C43, C51, D37, E17
University of Leeds: B133
University of Manitoba: F83, F173
University of New South Wales (Australia): D64
University of Oregon: D107
University of Pittsburgh study: C35, F184, F185, F192, F224
University of Tennessee at Knoxville: D102, F218
University of Toronto: E20, E36
University of Utah: E16
University of Virginia: E13
University of Windsor: B38
University of Wisconsin-Oshkosh: F2
University of Wisconsin System: F73
University related collections: A30
Use per monetary unit: C37
User charges: C39
User frustration: B25

Vendor selection: B32, B33, B36
Vertebrate zoology collections: F53
Virginia Beach Dept. of Public Libraries: E24
Virginia Polytechnic Institute: F155
VisiCalc: B85
Volumes per bibliographic volume: F28
VTLS system: E44

WLN (Washington Library
    Network): D74, D87,
    E50
Weeding: C70, C71, F111,
    F113, F123
Weeding periodicals: C70
Wellington Public Library
    (New Zealand): F82
Western Carolina University:
    B126, B129
Western Interstate Library
    Coordinating Organization
    (WILCO): A25, A42
Women's studies collections:
    E1
Working papers collections:
    F21

Yale University: G1

Zipf distribution: F211